EXCAVATING
BIBLE
TREASURES

Letting God Speak to Our Hearts Through His Word

HANNA SHAHIN, PH.D.

endureinternational.org

Excavating Bible Treasures: Letting God's
Word Speak to Our Hearts

Cover and Interior Design: Jennifer Poferl
Contributing Editor: Woodeene Koenig-Bricker
Cover art: stef ~/freeimages.com
ISBN: 9798640783377
1. Scripture 2. God's Word 3. Spiritual Reflections
First Edition

To Evelyn, my wife and ministry
partner for over 48 years and going.
Your encouragement, your gentle
prodding to keep me writing, and your
dedication to the Word of God continue
to be a source of inspiration to me.

CONTENTS

Introduction

By the middle of 1972, I had earned degrees in both philosophy and psychology and graduated from seminary, yet I still was a very lousy preacher. My appointment by my church leadership as a Sunday evening once-in-a-month-or-two preacher was a burdensome appointment. It was assumed that being a seminary graduate was all it took to turn someone like myself into a preacher. The fact is, it didn't. If someone had heard me preach my first sermonette in Jerusalem when I was 18 years old, it would not have sounded too much different from my preaching at the Beirut church in the early to mid-seventies, except for its shortness.

One year before graduating from seminary, I was offered a job at the Baptist Center for Radio and Television in Beirut, Lebanon. Our offices were adjacent to the seminary, at one end of the basement of their main building. So, once I was appointed a preacher at my church, I had continued access to the seminary library on the first floor. A couple of flights of stairs and I would be there, rampaging through all sorts of Bible commentaries, cutting and pasting a hastily compounded message, and then getting ready to present it within the next day or two. But even with such a vast reservoir of books, it was very challenging to decide what book of the Bible, and what chapter and verse, I should be preaching on.

I was a radio speaker, entertainer, and interviewer, but not a church preacher. The one and only time I began to seriously think of what portion of Scripture would best deal with our church family, I was led to a passage in the Old Testament—thankfully, I do not even recall which passage—which was judgmental in nature. I had been thinking for months that our church was becoming Pharisaical in nature, making rigid demands on women by decreeing how many centimeters below their knees their dresses should be. Another regulation decreed that except for medical reasons, women should not have their hair cut or dyed or extra hair removed from their faces or arms or eyebrows, while at the same time, little or no attention was paid to true holy living. We had become not a Spirit-filled church, but a prideful, self-centered church that looked down on sister churches and on their preachers.

For that one fateful message, I did not turn to any Bible commentary because I was about to present the State of the Church message. For my message, I spent hours in prayer, asking for insight, boldness, and wisdom. I knew this would be a make-it-or-break-it message. Either it would be received with humility and humbleness on the part of the church leadership, or my days there would be numbered!

I do not recall having such silence in the church auditorium as I did that evening. With a calm voice, I delivered my message. My heart was pounding heavily inside my chest, but somehow I managed to control it for the duration of my 20-minute message.

As I stood by the door to shake the hands of the worshippers as was customary, my heart was still pounding heavily. The sentencing could come sooner than expected. I might be called to the senior pastor's office the next day. He could deliver his verdict right there and then. His decision would seal my fate. Thankfully, I did not have to wait even that long. Our senior pastor did not mince his words. As he shook my hand, he told me I would have to share any future message with him to get his approval before I would be allowed to the pulpit again. Censorship! Biblical and spiritual censorship! My fears had come true. That would be my last message preached at that church. A year later, my family and I would be evacuating Lebanon because of the civil war and heading to Egypt.

The few years between my proper seminary training and the messages I preached in Beirut were solid proof that I was not made or meant to be a preacher. Even today, I do not look at myself as a preacher. For one, a preacher should be a good orator, and I am not, except on rare occasions. I was trained in and practiced radio speaking, talking, and interacting with my audiences for more than twenty-eight years of my life, not preaching at them. I challenged myself during those years, while sitting before a microphone in my studio in Beirut or Monte Carlo, to imagine myself sitting next to my listeners in their homes or in their cars and talking to them. Why should I be screaming, like some preachers tend to do, and scare my audience away? That continues to be my philosophy when I am asked to preach today.

My in-laws were living in a town 100 kilometers south of Cairo. The town was mid-sized and had a number of churches. Were it not for the fact that my in-laws were active Christians and quite well known, our family's temporary move from bustling Beirut to that town would have gone unnoticed. Nobody had heard my name there before. As importantly, nobody had a clue that I was a lousy preacher, or that the one time I preached a proper

Bible message, I was basically forced to leave that church. What church pastor in his right mind would invite me to his church? Yet, bad surprises can and do happen. In early January of 1976, I received an invitation to be a revival preacher at a local church. That meant preaching daily for one whole week. It was a hassle preaching once every month or two at the Beirut Church! Plus, I had a whole seminary library to help me back then. In my heart, I wanted to decline. The reasons were more than obvious. But doing so would shame my in-laws, because a seminary graduate was supposed to be able to preach. So here I was, stuck with no room, reason, or good excuse to say "no thanks." I agreed, but only after taking two weeks to prepare.

My father-in-law kept a small collection of books about Scripture that had been translated from English into Arabic, and a much smaller number authored by Arabs. I started by looking into his collection, hoping to find something that might help. I was back to my old ways, but not a single title jumped out at me. There was nothing between me and the pulpit of that church now except the Bible and my knees. So, almost grudgingly, I began by closing myself in the living room, going on my knees, reading the Bible, and praying. I would spend between seven and eight hours a day seeking the Lord's face, asking for understanding.

To this day, I cannot explain what happened. I did not have a vision, nor did I have a dream. But surprisingly, on the tenth day of my private time with God and the Word, it was as if scales fell off my heart and eyes, and I could begin to see the richness of the Word like never before. Until that morning, the Word had been enigmatic to me. I had not been able to see beyond the actual letters and the words they formed, which to me, represented black ink on white pages of paper. But now, those letters and words were breathing life. Those were no longer dead but living words, and I would be honored and privileged to share them with this church body.

The initial invitation was for one week, but it got extended into another week, and another week. Thirteen weeks in a row, I presented a new daily message from the Word of God, sometimes speaking at more than one church on a single day. I knew that this was not of my doing.

Years after this experience, my family and I would find ourselves serving in Africa, where a brother introduced us to a new method of studying the Bible: Inductive Bible Study (IBS). As I look back, I realize that this was actually what I was doing in my in-laws' living room as I poured out my heart and soul before the Lord and took time to read and re-read the Word, allowing it to take root and bring life and light. I may not have followed the same pattern or four steps of IBS, yet the end result was the same.

You are now holding a handbook in which I have collected a number of reflections on biblical passages that I have studied extensively over the years, and that I have presented to different audiences, from Morocco to Singapore and many countries in between. I owe special thanks to my older brother Salem, who heard me present some of these either at his church or to him in person and has "harassed" me to get them published for a wider audience.

I therefore humbly present what I have called *Excavating Bible Treasures*, seeking, above everything else, to whet the reader's appetite afresh for the Word of God and its richness. My wife, Evelyn, comes from Egypt, one of the great archaeological centers of the world. The treasures of that ancient world can be found everywhere. You can go out in the desert and kick aside a few stones and uncover a piece of pottery or even a bead or a bit of glass. It doesn't take much effort to find something. But if you want to uncover the real treasures, you have to excavate carefully and systematically. You have to devote time, effort, and energy. This reminded me of the Word of God. Merely tapping the soil may unearth a few interesting items. But for the real treasures, one has to excavate. If one wants to discover the richness of the Word of God, it is necessary to dig deep, therefore the title: *Excavating Bible Treasures.*

Finally, I have celebrated more than fifty years of walking with God. But that does not mean that I have enjoyed the richness of the Word all along the way. I have not. At many points in my journey, I have allowed myself to become apathetic toward the Word. I have read it and re-read it to the point of total familiarity, and familiarity breeds contempt. So, I present this humble collection with a sincere prayer that a new wave of zeal for the Word that will find its way into your soul and heart. May our prayer be like that of David when he wrote in Psalm 119:18, "Open my eyes that I may see wonderful things in your Law!"

god vs. God
I Believe in JHVH God

GENESIS 2:4

The attentive student of the Hebrew Bible, which Christians commonly call the Old Testament, will notice a startling change in the way God is presented in the first three chapters of the Book of Genesis. Beginning at Genesis 1:1, the reader is introduced to the Creator by a single word: God, *Elohim* in Hebrew. The same word is repeated thirty times in 31 verses throughout that chapter. We come across that same single word three times in Chapter 2:2–3.

But then, beginning at Genesis 2:4, we come across an additional term preceding the word *God*. That word in the Hebrew original is the personal name of God, namely *JHVH*. It now seems that the writer of the Book of Genesis is introducing us to the specific God who created the heavens and the earth and everything there is. The writer did this, it appears, to make sure that the reader does not give any credit to other gods. The creator of the universe is not any god. He is JHVH God.

The first part of chapter 3, verse 1 informs us again of the identity of the Creator God by clearly stating his name: JHVH. Yet when the serpent (Satan) begins addressing Eve, he omits the specific name of God and refers to him simply by the word "God." Eve follows suit and does exactly the same thing in her answer, and the serpent does it twice more.

Is such an omission significant? And if so, how significant?

Before I answer that question, it is worthwhile noting that the term *Elohim* in Hebrew is not an exclusive term that necessarily refers to JHVH God. *Elohim*—or *god* in English—is a common noun that was used to refer to diverse gods. There are ample references to this in Scripture. For example, Exodus 20:3 states, "You shall have no other gods (*Elohim*) before me."

The term for "gods" in Hebrew is the same term that is used of God in Genesis 1:1; namely, *Elohim*. After "Moses told his father-in-law about everything the Lord had done to Pharaoh and the Egyptians for Israel's sake and about all the hardships they had met along the way and how the Lord had saved them" (Exodus 18:8), his father-in-law Jethro says, "Now I know that the Lord is greater than all other gods" (Exodus 18:11a). The Hebrew term for "all gods" is *Elohim*. We come across that term scores of times in the Hebrew Bible, referring to a multitude of gods that different peoples worshipped at different times. The reason behind its widespread usage is simply that it is a common noun, whereas the name JHVH very specifically refers to the God of Abraham, Isaac, and Jacob.

It is also worth noting that there are multiple instances in the Hebrew Bible in which followers of JHVH God refer to him simply by the term *Elohim* without stating his proper name JHVH. What are we to make of that?

First, the Jewish followers of the Law were taught to avoid using God's proper name. Therefore, we, as non-Jews, cannot use Jewish teaching as a reason to fail to use God's proper name. The followers of the Law knew whom they were speaking of or speaking to without the need to use his proper name. The same can never be used as an argument for those who do not follow the Jewish Law.

It has been said that the term *Elohim* in its reference to JHVH God refers mostly to his creative power, whereas JHVH refers to a personal relationship he had with his followers. There may be quite a bit of truth in this statement. However, not every occurrence of the term *Elohim* refers to God's creative power, and not every occurrence of his proper name JHVH refers to his personal relationship with people.

Now back to our passage in Genesis 3, and the question of how significant Satan's omission of God's proper name was in his interaction with Eve that eventful day. By omitting God's proper name, Satan was making JHVH God just another god. That explains the basis of his promise to Eve that she and Adam would be like *god*. JHVH was nothing special in Satan's eyes. Man and woman could easily become gods like *god*. Sadly, Eve fell for the bait. She also omits using the name of God in her answer. To her, JHVH God becomes just another god, and she now wants to become like him.

Based on this interpretation, we can surmise that since Satan did not have a personal relationship with JHVH God, he couldn't possibly use God's proper name. Not only that, but Satan also misleads Eve to do the same, thus paving the way for a disconnect between JHVH God and humanity.

When did Eve's fall begin? Was it when she looked at the fruit of that tree? Was it when she spoke to Satan and allowed him to mislead her? I am not of either opinion. Eve could have looked at the tree all day long without picking any of its fruit. She could also have chatted with Satan and not fallen for his bait. I think the Fall started the moment Eve omitted the name of God JHVH from her vocabulary. For it is then that JHVH became just another god that she believed she could become like.

Eve's fall began when she omitted the proper name of God and thus ruptured her relationship with JHVH God. It is then that Eve and Adam decided to go their own way. Going one's own way—apart from God—is what sin really means. It is the desire for independence from JHVH God.

Have things changed since that fateful day? Sadly not. God is just another god to many people in the world today. They claim to believe in god. And they do. They may even refer to him as *Elohim,* but that does not necessarily mean JHVH God. As for me, I don't believe in *god.* I believe in JHVH God.

CHAPTER 2

"God Walking"
When God Is with Us

GENESIS 3:8–10

If I were to ask ten Bible students to look at Genesis 3 and choose one verse that jumps out at them, my guess is that they might choose any verse except verse 8, especially the first part of that verse. Yet for me, this verse stands out more than any other.

To understand why, let us read Genesis 3:8–10 in context. We pick up the story of Adam and Eve after they had listened to the tempter and eaten of the forbidden tree. They have realized their nakedness and covered themselves with fig leaves before going into hiding.

> Then the man and his wife heard the sound of the Lord God as he was walking in the garden in the cool of the day, and they hid from the Lord God among the trees of the garden. But the Lord God called to the man, "Where are you?" He answered, "I heard you in the garden, and I was afraid because I was naked; so I hid." (Genesis 3:8–10)

A Bible student may ask why I choose verse 8 as my favorite since there are clearly more central verses in this chapter. I generally agree. As a matter of fact, there is so much going on in this chapter, almost as if it sums up the whole Bible story and the whole history of humanity. This chapter consists of only 24 verses (just over 700 words), yet it covers the disobedience of humanity, the judgment of God, the promise of redemption, and the divorce of earth from heaven and humanity from God. Yet, verse 8 is still my favorite verse, at least for this study. And if I were to pick just two words from that verse, they would be "God walking." I realize I need to explain myself.

In the first two chapters of Genesis, we mostly hear God speaking. The words "And God said" occur several times in chapter 1. In chapter 2, God put Adam in the Garden of Eden and gave him orders on what to eat and what not to eat.

The uniqueness of the words "God walking" in chapter 3 is that this is the first occasion when God shows up not to give orders, but to have an honest discussion with the man and woman he created. The first two chapters of Genesis are silent as to whether God had times of fellowship or discussion with Adam and Eve before this occasion. Since Adam and Eve recognized God by the sound of his steps, it would not be completely out of the question to assume that they had had previous conversations or encounters with him. Yet, that remains an assumption, not a certainty.

So, this is the first recorded time that God comes to meet Adam and Eve in the garden that had become their home. But, that is not what makes verse 8 unique. Rather, it is unique because God is walking on his two feet, so to speak. With the power, authority, and energy his voice carried, God had created the heavens and the earth and all that is. But now, it is as if he takes on human flesh and blood. He comes walking.

In Genesis 2:7 we read that "the Lord God formed a man from the dust of the ground and breathed into his nostrils," which would suppose that God used his hands to form that man and used his mouth to breathe into his nostrils. But here again, this is only an assumption. Genesis 2 does not provide these details. But here in Genesis 3:8, we have the word "walking," which we cannot interpret in any other way except that God was actually walking on two feet!

While it is easy to imagine God having mud on his hands as he formed humanity from the dust of the earth, now he has mud on his feet as well. How could he lift "man" from his "muddy" situation unless he came down to where "man" was and had his own feet in the mud?

One might argue that this could be the first divine incarnation in Scripture. It may well be. To me, though, this is the first time God is presented as an approachable God. He could have again used his voice without appearing on the scene. But no, this is not a distant God who chooses to talk to his creation from within the clouds of heaven. He is approachable and personable.

God is on a mission to see and seek humanity. He does not ask Adam and Eve to meet him halfway. God goes all the way to where they are. He walks to meet them where he can hear their hearts beat, where he can check their rapid pulses and see the fear in their eyes. He does not knock the tree down where Adam and Eve are hiding. He comes walking as a friend. God is no intruder. If there had been a gate to the Garden, he would have rung the bell to be allowed to go in.

Equally important, God was in no hurry. This is why we see him walking. He knew what had happened, and so he could have passed judgment without discussing the ins and outs of what Adam and Eve had done. But God was concerned for Adam and for Eve, and so he takes the time to talk with them and be involved with them.

Humanity's fall became God's chief concern. He had to get involved. Adam and Eve knew what to do to get into trouble, but they did not know how to get out of it. One would imagine that since they were the ones to disobey, they would be the ones to seek after God in an attempt to rectify things. And if they did not know where to find him, the least they could have done when they heard him was to rush to him and confess what they had done. Instead, they hid. Even then, God did not confront them. Friends do not confront. With love, they lead the other party to confess by asking questions. This is what God did as a loving friend to Adam and Eve.

It is quite striking to compare God's reaction to the disobedience of Adam and Eve with how he communicated with Cain when he killed his brother Abel. In the first instance, God came walking to spend time with Adam and Eve before pronouncing judgment and then promising redemption while covering their nakedness. In the second, he simply pronounced Cain cursed. God was on a mission of redemption in the case of Adam and Eve, but not so in passing judgment on Cain.

If Almighty God took on himself the trouble of walking to where Adam and Eve's sin had dragged them, then the least he expects of us—we who are fallen sinners saved by grace—is to remember our own past, to humble ourselves, and to feel for and touch our fellow sinners in their situations. God has set an example for us in Genesis 3:8. As his sons and daughters, we are called upon to follow that example. He has set the only true standard of what Christian mission and Christian ministry, in general, should be like.

Christian mission is always about redemption. Christian mission should always be incarnational, walking to meet "man" where fallen "man" is. It never stops with the warning of judgment. It consists of walking, even in our fallen state, getting a better handle on the circumstances of sin, and offering the antidote. Christian mission is not confrontational. It seeks to understand and empathize rather than rush to pronounce judgment. Christian mission is an investment of time and a promise of redemption, hope, and a better day when paradise will be gained again. Christian mission is walking in the muddy lanes of this fallen world to reach down and help lift our brothers and sisters from their muddy situation. If God took on himself to come down walking to meet humanity where humanity dwelt, how much more should we be willing to do the same!

CHAPTER 3

What's in a Letter?
A More Literal Translation

GENESIS 4:10

As a student of the Bible, I often go back to the original text, whether in Hebrew or in Greek, but always with the help of the corresponding interlinear texts in order to better grasp the meaning of a word, a phrase, or a name. I also read multiple English translations with the hope that someone else has done their homework to the fullest and thus saved me time from doing my own research. Although there are cases in which this has been true, often what appears to a translator to be either insignificant or too obvious to mention can conceal a treasure trove of meaning and thus great potential impact. One such case is in Genesis 4:10. Here is its rendition according to the NIV: "The Lord said, 'What have you done? Listen! Your brother's blood cries out to me from the ground.'"

The one word that caught my attention was "blood," because in the Hebrew original, that word is in the plural—"bloods"—and not in the singular form as we have it in English and other translations. So, what's in a letter? What difference can the letter "s" make? Moreover, how many "bloods" did Abel have? Or did the recorder of the events of the Book of Genesis mistakenly add a letter? If not that writer, what about the scribes who followed?

The fact is that neither the individual who recorded the Book of Genesis nor the scribes copying it made any mistakes. And while it is true that Abel as a person, like all of us, had blood in the singular, that missing letter results in our missing a very important message.

What was God saying when he used the word *bloods*? Before getting into that, let me give the following example. If I were to hold in my hand one grain of wheat or one grain of barley, you could rightly argue that in its present state, I am holding only a single grain. Yet, looking into the future, that one grain has the potential of becoming a billion grains. As the one grain grows and produces other grains, and as those other grains grow and produce more grains, over time, there would be more grains than any calculator would be able to count.

If, on the other hand, rather than planting that one grain, you were to crush it and throw it away, you could be rightly accused of wasting not one single and simple grain, but billions and billions of grains. You have taken away that one grain's potential to bring forth all the other grains.

Now to the question of "bloods." When Cain slew Abel, he was not spilling the blood of one individual. He was, in fact, denying Abel the potential of bringing into the world generations of humans. Thus, he was spilling the "bloods" of those potential generations. Could that be the reason why that word appears in the plural form? What more serious sin could there be than destroying untold generations?

In today's economy, killing another human being has become

trivial. Such a crime does not carry the weighty responsibility that God seems to be placing on it from the beginning of human history. It may be for this very reason that, according to the Law of Moses, the punishment for murder was nothing less than death for the perpetrator. For in the same way that Cain denied Abel his future generations, a murderer denies the victim not only a personal individual life but also all the victim's potential progeny. Death as the punishment for murder likewise denies the murderer his or her future generations.

May we value human life as God values it, regardless of race, religion, or ethnicity. Because we are all the sons and daughters of Adam and Eve, we are no less siblings than were Cain and Abel.

CHAPTER 4

Our True Abode
Enoch, The First Biblical City

GENESIS 4:11–17

Some cities are absolutely gorgeous! The streets are well lit. The sidewalks are clean. The directions and signs are all in big, bold letters, and even a foreign visitor can find it hard to get lost. These cities have excellent drainage systems. Buses and public transport have their lanes and so do private cars. Speed limits are well controlled. Skyscrapers may well hide the sun even in the middle of the day, but they add their beauty and marvelous design. Singapore is one such city. Monte Carlo is another, with others in Europe, the United States, and elsewhere in the world. They are marvels to visit and enjoy!

Sadly, there are other cities in which nothing seems to be in order. Neither cars nor pedestrians respect traffic lights. There are no proper drainage systems, and rain causes flooding. Add to that the misery of pollution or overcrowdedness, and you will want to avoid going to these cities.

But whether cities are beautiful or ugly, one thing is common. They have just about everything one might need, whether for business or for pleasure. One does not need to go outside the city to find a bakery or a plumber, or anything in between. It is all there. Cities are a convenient place to live.

So, what is wrong with building a city or with living in one? On the surface, there is nothing wrong, unless a city is built with an ulterior motive, or unless it hides an attitude of self-defiance and self-satisfaction! Before we discuss this further, let us turn to Genesis 4:11–17. We pick up the story after Cain kills his brother Abel and God pronounces his judgment. Because of his deed, Cain was to be a restless wanderer. God's earth would not welcome him anymore, anywhere. His fate had been decided for him. He would live a nomadic life.

Cain pleads his losing case before the Lord, but he is scared for his life. Although he does acknowledge that he will be hidden from the presence of God, meaning cut out of fellowship with God, that is not his main or real concern. Instead, he is concerned that whoever finds him will kill him. It makes one wonder why he thought it was okay to kill his brother, but not okay for someone else to kill him.

In his graciousness, the Lord puts a mark on Cain so that no one would kill him. Despite that, Cain shows no remorse for what he did. There is no admission of wrongdoing or sin. There is no repentance or plea for forgiveness. It is all about himself. That mark should have reminded Cain of the goodness of God who gave him a second chance at life. If anything, that mark was a living testimony of God in his life. It should have guided him to seek God again and ask forgiveness. But, instead, Cain and his wife went to live in the land of Nod, east of Eden, and, in total defiance of God and of his judgment, Cain started building a city. He called that city Enoch.

A city represents self-satisfaction. A city represents independence and interdependence, as well as arrogance and, in some ways, contentment. By building the city, Cain was basically saying to God, "I do not need you anymore. You cut me out of fellowship with you, so I am cutting you out of my life and the life of my family. I am building a city and even putting a wall around it. You are out. Stay out!"

Humanity has continued building cities ever since that first city called Enoch was built. Yet the truth is that we do not need to build an actual city to express our independence from God, our defiance toward God, or our self-satisfaction and contentment. In that sense, we have become our own cities. Each one of us can be a city unto ourselves. We have no more need for God in our lives. We can take care of ourselves, with science, technology, medical research, and much more giving us independence, or so we think. Pretty soon, we may assume the power to create life on our own, completely keeping God out of the picture. We do not need a God in the city or in our lives.

We think of a nomad as someone who does not have a stable abode or a place to call home. When we become independent of God, we become nomads. We may have an abode here on earth, but it is a temporary abode. One day we will move away and leave an empty space that another nomad will fill. Our true and eternal home is elsewhere. It is God's desire that we make his abode ours as well. It is God's will that we take down the walls that we have built around our lives and the false sense of security that we have erected and turn back to him. Only in him are we ever secure and safe.

Where is the city called Enoch that Cain built? Scholars and archaeologists have no idea. We cannot even find one remaining stone of that city. Its walls and its foundations have all crumbled. That city only provided a temporary and false sense of security and safety to Cain and his family. Is there a lesson or two here for us?

By Any Other Name
Name or Testimony?

GENESIS 11:2–8

The concept of names fills the Bible from its very first pages. God gives Adam his name, and Adam gives Eve her name. Gradually, we are introduced to a host of names, including *Noah, Abraham, Isaac, Jacob*, and too many others to count.

Names are how we are known and identified, and how we come to know other people. Some people may be identified by additional aspects, such as their beauty, wisdom, or patience. Names will often conjure up images in our imaginations. For instance, if you ask who in the Bible suffered greatly by losing his property and family, yet would not curse God, the name of Job would instantly spring to mind. We have come to know Job by these different aspects of his life.

This is true not just of Bible characters, but of family members, important people in our lives, and political and social leaders. Literature, the media, and word of mouth all shape the images that invade our minds. Books, magazines, and newspapers, as well as radio, television, and the internet, are powerful tools that shape our thinking and our imaginations, so much so that the mere mention of a name may create either a positive or negative mental reaction. For example, the name "Abraham Lincoln" may automatically create a positive connotation in the listener's mind. In contrast, the name "Adolf Hitler" may automatically elicit a negative reaction.

My question as we look at names is simple: Why did the Bible writers and the Spirit of God behind them choose to mention the names of some individuals, with the images they conjure up, and remain completely obscure as to the names of others? For example, what is the name of Job's wife? She leaves a negative image in our minds when she says, "Are you still maintaining your integrity? Curse God and die!" (Job 2:9). But is that negative statement the reason why her name is not disclosed? Obviously not, since we have quite a few other negative and evil biblical characters whose names have been recorded and passed down to us, such as Jeroboam and Judas Iscariot. Could it be because she was a woman, and the writers of the Bible didn't feel it important to name women? That also is untrue, since we have many named women—including the evil Jezebel—and many unnamed men.

We may remember the commander of the army of Aram, who was struck with leprosy. We may also recall the prophet who told him to dip himself in the River Jordan seven times. These two men are Naaman and Elisha, respectively. But what was the name of the enslaved Israelite girl who suggested to Naaman's (unnamed) wife that the prophet in Samaria could cure Naaman's leprosy? She remained anonymous.

How about the Samaritan woman who became the first home missionary? She also remained nameless. And how about the name of the Good Samaritan! Why did Jesus not tell us who that was? We also have the unnamed centurion who witnessed the Crucifixion of the Lord and the nameless Ethiopian eunuch who was led to faith in Christ by Philip's witness to him. And let us not forget the jailer and all his household who came to faith upon seeing the power of God proclaimed through the testimony of Paul and Silas, according to Acts 16.

I do not know why some names were spelled out and others were not. However, there is an important lesson for us to learn from anonymous Bible characters. I ask you, what is really more important, one's name or one's testimony? What is more important, Naaman's wife's slave's name or her bold testimony to the God of Israel? The name of the Samaritan woman or her witness that led many to believe? The name of the Good Samaritan or his deeds? The name of the centurion or the amazing testimony he gave after surviving the earthquake, saying, "Surely he was the Son of God" (Matthew 27:54)? The names of the eunuch and the jailer or their conversion stories? Names can mislead or be forgotten, but a testimony cannot.

I do not mean to be judgmental. I also do not mean to do away with all our names. Having said that, I believe it is about time that we begin a discussion on the whole culture of "name-making." We live in a culture that glorifies names, leading many to seek with all our might to make a name for ourselves. This is true in almost every arena of our world, whether in sports, politics, science, or entertainment. Sadly, Christians have not been spared. Authors—myself included—want to be remembered. Preachers also want to be remembered! Perhaps we all want to be remembered by name!

Our calling, if I understand the Scriptures correctly, is to make a name for Christ and not for ourselves. It is his name that ought to be proclaimed, not ours. It is his name that ought to receive glory, not ours. And the way we do that is by and through a genuine Christian testimony.

The Apostle Paul gives us an example to follow. Who has not heard of him, regardless of the images that are drawn up in our minds when his name is mentioned? Knowing the trap that could be set for him with the name God made for him, he made sure to always point to Christ rather than to himself. We hear him challenging the church at Corinth with the following exhortation: "For I resolved to know nothing while I was with you except Jesus Christ and him crucified" (1 Corinthians 2:2). And again, he wrote, "What, after all, is Apollos? And what is Paul? Only servants, through whom you came to believe, as the Lord has assigned to each his task" (1 Corinthians 3:5).

Names are and will continue to be essential. But name-making is not. The choice is ours to make. We will either work to have a name for ourselves, or we will work to make the name of Christ known.

CHAPTER 6

Fathers and Sons
When Analogies Fail

GENESIS 22:1–14

Some images in Scripture force their analogies on us to the point at which we stop looking any more deeply. This is true especially when such images have made their way to preachers' platforms. By then, if we had any doubts about what analogy a specific image could imply, the messages we hear only help to reinforce the given analogy we already have, and from that point on, we stop examining the image. We find one of those images in the story of Abraham and Isaac.

I cannot count the times I've heard or read that Abraham's relationship to Isaac points to the relationship in the Godhead between Father and Son. Before we examine the analogy, I encourage you to first read the entire text for yourself in Genesis 22:1–14.

In verse 2, we read, "Take your son, your only son, whom you love." Our minds immediately travel to occasions in the New Testament in which Jesus is also called an only Son, and a beloved Son at that. By simply looking at the unique relationship that tied Abraham to his son Isaac, it is fairly easy to see an image of the Father's unique relationship with the Son. Isaac was an only son (leaving aside Ishmael, whom Abraham had fathered with Hagar) and he was the beloved son.

In John 1:14, 1:18, 3:16, and 3:18, Jesus is designated as the only Son. Then, at his baptism by John the Baptist, the Father called out from heaven proclaiming, "This is my Son, whom I love; with him I am well pleased" (Matthew 3:17).

With such strong emphasis on Abraham's love relationship with his only son, Isaac, and with the same type of emphasis on the Father's love relationship with his only Son, Jesus, the idea is already in place. We draw conclusions and set the analogy in concrete. Abraham represents God the Father, and Isaac represents God the Son. Abraham is to sacrifice his son, and the Father will also offer his Son as a sacrifice.

Such analogy, or representation, begs one important question: Did Abraham actually offer his son? Did he drive the knife into his son's heart and kill him? The answer is obviously no, he didn't. The analogy breaks down with this first question because Jesus did die on the Cross. The Father allowed his head to be crowned with thorns, his hands and feet to be nailed to a cross, and his side to be pierced. Very much unlike Isaac, who got out of the incident shaken but unscratched, Jesus died and was buried.

To counter this argument, some biblical commentators and expositors turn to Hebrews 11:17–19:

> By faith, Abraham, when God tested him, offered Isaac as a sacrifice. He who had embraced the promises was about to sacrifice his one and only

son, even though God had said to him, "It is through Isaac that your offspring will be reckoned." Abraham reasoned that God could even raise the dead, and so in a manner of speaking he did receive Isaac back from death.

Some expositors emphasize verse 19; that is, the idea that, to Abraham, the rescue was like receiving Isaac "back from death." The author of Hebrews is saying that Abraham had such strong faith in God that he believed that if he had actually killed Isaac, God would have raised him up. Abraham's actions were based on that faith. God had promised Abraham that he would have a lineage, or descendants through Isaac. Therefore, even if he killed his son, God would raise him up.

The author of the Letter to the Hebrews never intended to make Isaac a representation or analogy of Jesus. We cannot stretch the words to make them say things they do not. The context does not lend itself to such wild speculation.

The analogy between Abraham and Isaac and the Father and Jesus is erroneous and perverted. Simply stated, it goes against the "faith" principle that is so central to biblical theology in both Testaments. Ever since the days of Cain and Abel, God made it very clear that he would not accept human labor as worship. This principle is first outlined in Genesis and runs through the rest of the Bible. God refused the fruits of human labor as presented by Cain. (See Genesis 4:2–5.) Cain "worked the soil" and then brought the fruits of the soil as an offering to God.

How did God look at the fruits of Cain's labor? Did these find favor with God? Did they gain Cain access to God's throne? The answer is obviously negative. Not only was there no actual sacrifice, but what Cain offered was works-based worship, which has no merit before God.

Similarly, Isaac is the fruit of Abraham's and Sarah's labor. We would be completely wrong to believe that a sacrifice of labor would please God, but even more in error to think that a human sacrifice would ever please God. Human sacrifice was one reason why God brought down judgment on the peoples living in Canaan at the time. They were offering their sons and daughters as burnt sacrifices.

So here again, a representation or analogy comparing the sacrifice of Abraham with the sacrifice of the Father is not worth the ink or paper it is written with or on, with all due respect to Bible commentators and expositors. God never intended for us to offer our sons and daughters. Isaiah 64:6 says, "our righteous acts are like filthy rags." Why would God want a filthy rag as an offering?

Now to a second question relating to this faulty analogy. Where does the ram fit in this representation? If Isaac represents Jesus, what does the ram represent? We cannot simply ignore the ram and hope no one notices it. Here again with the ram, the analogy of comparing Abraham with the Father and Isaac with Jesus breaks down.

Such a faulty analogous comparison throws the whole Christian redemption story out the window. In fact, it supports heretical views that maintain that someone else—such as Judas Iscariot or Simon of Cyrene—actually died during the Crucifixion, while Jesus was lifted up to heaven. If this is true, then the Jews and the Romans all got it wrong: Jesus was saved and someone else died in his place. Such a theology reflects what the Father/Son analogy claims: Isaac never died, and, similarly, Jesus never died.

If we are to use the story of Abraham in Genesis 22 in an analogous depiction, Abraham would represent humanity in our attempts to please God by offering him the fruits of our labor represented by Isaac. Instead, God provides the lamb or ram that will redeem Isaac and grant him life. That ram had to be put to death. Judgment fell on the ram.

There are two things to keep in mind here. First, salvation is God's handiwork. Redemption was in the heart of God from before the creation of the world. It was heaven reaching down to earth and providing a means of reconciliation and not earth petitioning heaven. This is the glory of the Christian faith. It is not and has never been humanity's vain attempts at pleasing God or reaching up to him. Salvation only comes from God.

Secondly, it is the ram and not Isaac that would represent or resemble Christ in his death. The Old Testament is replete with images of lambs being slaughtered as sacrifices until the coming of the perfect Lamb of God, who will take away the sins of the world.

We do the Word of God and ourselves an injustice, and we promote bad theology, when our study of the Bible is not done carefully. There is nothing wrong with an analogy based on Bible parables or images, but such an analogy should be in complete harmony with the biblical message of the grace of God, and not of the works of man.

CHAPTER 7

The Shema
Orthodoxy vs. Orthopraxy

DEUTERONOMY 6:4–5

No prayer is more central to Judaism than the Shema, which is based on Deuteronomy 6:4–5: "Hear, O Israel: The Lord our God, the Lord is one. Love the Lord your God with all your heart and with all your soul and with all your strength." For many Jewish worshippers, verse 4, the affirmation that God is one, is most important, for it reflects their monotheism.

The main reason for my "excavating" into this verse has to do with the Hebrew term "אחד," which is usually translated as "one." Yet, these three letters can also mean "only" or even "alone." So, we must ask the question: Does the Shema indicate Jewish belief in one God from the very beginning?

Before I go any further, allow me to elucidate by looking at the literal meaning of the Jewish term for God, JHVH, which means the Ever Present, or the I AM. This name is unique and exclusive and thus one. No other gods had that name except the God of Israel. But, on the other hand, the word "Lord" is a translation of the Hebrew term *Adonai*. If that term is used, it might be argued that there could be many lords or even multiple gods, but, for the Jews, the pronoun "our" indicates worship of only one God.

Thus, it is possible that the Shema may not be conclusive proof of early Jewish monotheism. I do not mean that Jewish worshippers didn't believe in the oneness of God. Yet from a more exegetical viewpoint, monotheism is not necessarily the theme here. One important reason is that the Hebrew Bible testifies to the existence of many other gods. Consider Exodus 20:1–3: "And God spoke all these words: 'I am the Lord your God, who brought you out of Egypt, out of the land of slavery. You shall have no other gods before me.'" God is explicitly and exclusively identifying himself and none other as the God of Israel. What God is not saying is that he is the only god. As a matter of fact, quite the contrary. If the Israelites didn't accept that there were other gods in existence, there would have been no need for God to proclaim himself the unique and only God for and of Israel. God would have been the only God recognized by all people. But, we know from the biblical witness that other peoples worshipped their own gods, and the Israelites recognized these gods as gods. Idolatry, which presupposes the existence and worship of more than one god or goddess, was the one sin that would be punished like no other.

Returning to the Shema, it is my opinion that the Shema is not so much a theological proclamation or affirmation of the oneness of God, but, rather, of the absolute singularity of JHVH God for the nation of Israel. He is the only God for them!

But that is not all. The Shema does not stop with verse 4. In the second part of the Shema, God was not simply revealing his exclusivity to his people. He was also expecting a certain behavior based on that revelation. In other words, God was not just in the business of teaching his people the correct doctrine that he was their only God. He expected them to be exclusively devoted to him. So as important as verse 4 was, so was the succeeding verse:

"Love the Lord your God with all your heart and with all your soul and with all your strength."

Why are there two parts? Because the Shema is not merely about orthodoxy, which literally means correct opinion or correct doctrine, but also about orthopraxy, or correct action. JHVH God chose to be the exclusive God of the Israelites (Jews), and he wants their total love and affection. The Shema thus presents both the doctrinal and the practical—God choosing to be their unique God, and his people choosing to love him with all their heart, soul, and strength.

Moving to the New Testament, consider Matthew 22:34–38:

> Hearing that Jesus had silenced the Sadducees, the Pharisees got together. One of them, an expert in the law, tested him with this question: "Teacher, which is the greatest commandment in the Law?" Jesus replied: "Love the Lord your God with all your heart and with all your soul and with all your mind." This is the first and greatest commandment.

What is so amazing, even strange, is that the Lord Jesus here simply addresses the latter part of the Shema and completely forgoes the first. This is not to mean in any way that he thought the first part was unimportant. Rather, it seems to indicate that our emphasis should rather be on the second part, on our role toward this God who has uniquely and exclusively chosen us to be his people.

My reflections are not directed at Jewish worshippers, but at us, as Christians, who believe in the God of Israel as the only God and have chosen to make him our only God. We may recognize God as the only God, but have we chosen to give him our full and complete devotion?

CHAPTER 8

Give or Lend
The Need for Correct Translation

1 SAMUEL 1:1–28

The two main recurring verbs that carry the story of Samuel in 1 Samuel 1:1–28 are "give" and "given," as in "So now I give him to the Lord. For his whole life he will be given over to the Lord" (1 Samuel 1:28). In fact, most translations use only these two specific words in their rendering of the Hebrew verb *shaool*. Since verbs often carry the meaning of a sentence, it becomes important to know what those verbs are and what they truly mean. In the case of *shaool*, the correct translation is "to lend," not "to give."

So, what difference does that make? Before answering this question, let us go back to the events leading to this "lending." We are told that Hannah, the wife of Elkanah, had no children. Hannah was deeply saddened by this, and one year, she prayed to the Lord and made this vow: "Lord Almighty, if you will only look on your servant's misery and remember me, and not forget your servant but give her a son, then I will give him to the Lord for all the days of his life, and no razor will ever be used on his head." (1 Samuel 1:11). Eventually, her prayer was heard, and she bore a son, Samuel. After he was weaned, she fulfilled her vow by giving him "over to the Lord" (1 Samuel 1:28).

In the NIV, as in most other translations, the word *shaool* is translated exclusively as "give." So, what difference does it make whether we use "give" or "lend?" To me, the difference is quite meaningful.

The first distinction is that "to give" is to hand over without expectation of return, but "to lend" is to grant the use of something with the anticipation that it will be returned at some point. If Hannah "gave" Samuel, she would not expect to see him again, but if she "lent" him, she would not see it as a final cutting of ties.

Then, we need to ask who is giving what to whom? Is Hannah giving Samuel to God, as she indicates in verse 11? Is it not God who gave Samuel to Hannah? Did she not pray and plead year after year that God may give her a son? So why is Hannah giving Samuel back to the Lord? The fact is that she isn't. She is lending him to the Lord!

The story of Hannah came to mind when I was asked to speak at the memorial service for the death of a friend's twenty-one-year-old son. Speaking at a memorial service is nobody's favorite hobby, and definitely not mine. What does one say that could bring comfort to a grieving mom and dad? I tried to excuse myself from the speaking request, but I could not. So, I thought and prayed for something meaningful, and I was reminded of Hannah and her offer to lend Samuel to the Lord. I wondered how long Samuel was going to live, and how long Hannah, his mother, was going to live. It made sense to me to think of God lending us our fathers and mothers, our brothers and sisters, and our sons and daughters. They are not ours; they are merely lent to us.

Such a mindset would lead us to live with a conscious understanding of whom we really belong to. We would live with the conscious realization that inasmuch as we do not own our own lives, we also do not own anybody else's. It follows that we cannot give anyone to anybody, not the least to God to whom everything belongs in the first place. He lends us our lives, but, in the end, we return them to him.

I do not know if my words to the grieving family made sense that day or provided any comfort. However, my conviction then and now is that unless we consciously live the conviction that we belong to God, every loss we experience will be magnified. When we lose those we love, the loss is even greater. The only answer to our losses is to graciously allow God to take anything and everything he has lent to us. We have never been owners of anything! We are only stewards, and stewards are required to be faithful to their stewardship, including the stewardship of life itself.

Human Uncleanness
Touching a Leper

MATTHEW 8:1–4

We read in Leviticus 5:3, 5 that "if they touch human uncleanness (anything that would make them unclean) even though they are unaware of it, but then they learn of it and realize their guilt ... when anyone becomes aware that they are guilty in any of these matters, they must confess in what way they have sinned."

Confronted with this clear Old Testament regulation concerning the clean and unclean, we find a puzzling situation in the life of Jesus in Matthew 8:1–4:

> When Jesus came down from the mountainside, large crowds followed him. A man with leprosy came and knelt before him and said, "Lord, if you are willing, you can make me clean."
>
> Jesus reached out his hand and touched the man. "I am willing," he said. "Be clean!" Immediately he was cleansed of his leprosy. Then Jesus said to him, "See that you don't tell anyone.

> But go, show yourself to the priest and offer the gift
> Moses commanded, as a testimony to them."

This was not the first time that Jesus would heal someone with leprosy. In Luke 17:11–19, Jesus heals ten lepers. But there is a huge difference between these two incidents, which means that we have a huge problem on our hands. Let me explain. In the case of the ten lepers, Jesus orders them to be clean from a distance. He does not touch them, and neither do they touch him. But in Matthew 8, the text is very clear and unambiguous: Jesus reached out and touched the man.

The Old Testament text from Leviticus is also clear and unambiguous. Two things happen to those who touch human uncleanness. First, they become unclean themselves, and second, they become guilty and will have to confess their sin.

So, how can we understand the text from Matthew? That Jesus became unclean or guilty is not permissible. We are talking of God incarnate. There must be other considerations.

One such consideration is that Jesus is above the Law. He is above what Leviticus dictates since he is the one dictating it. But then, how can someone dictate a law and then break it? Such a consideration is void.

Another consideration is that Jesus touched the man at a clean spot on his body where there was no sign of leprosy. But here again, that consideration does not hold much water. Uncleanness is not related to the affected spots in one's body. Either the person is clean or unclean. There is nothing half clean.

A third consideration would be to think of an authority much more powerful than that of leprosy, namely the authority to heal. In that sense, the authority that Jesus had within him was much more powerful than the man's uncleanness. This would explain how the man would be completely healed without Jesus being negatively affected.

Though such an interpretation sounds plausible, it would beg the question of why Jesus touched him at all. If Jesus did not touch the ten lepers, yet his authority over their sickness was enough to drive it away with his word, why not do the same here without raising such serious questions about uncleanness and guilt? This leaves this third consideration also lacking solid ground.

A fourth potential consideration is that Jesus defied the Law. This is the position of the famous commentator William Barclay. Barclay adds that while Jesus did defy the Law when he touched the leper, he made sure that the leper would then do exactly what the Law required; that is, going to a priest and then offering the gift as Moses commanded.

With all due respect to Mr. Barclay, it is inconceivable that in one instant Jesus would defy the Law, and, in the next, order the healed leper to follow that same Law. We know from the Sermon on the Mount that Jesus said he did not come to "abolish the Law or the Prophets" (Matthew 5:17). The verb "abolish" means to annul, void, or do away with. If Jesus was truly defying the Law, he would, in fact, be annulling it, voiding it, and doing away with it.

All four previous considerations have proven to be lacking and fallacious, which brings us back to one conclusion. When Jesus deliberately touched the leper, he was taking on himself both uncleanness and guilt. But is that permissible?

The answer, perhaps to the surprise of many, is a definite yes. Jesus was deliberately taking on the man's uncleanness and thus he himself became guilty. To better explain this position and interpretation, we turn to Isaiah 53:4–6:

> Surely he took up our pain and bore our
>   suffering,
> yet we considered him punished by God,
>   stricken by him, and afflicted.
> But he was pierced for our transgressions,

> he was crushed for our iniquities;
> the punishment that brought us peace was on him,
> and by his wounds we are healed.
> We all, like sheep, have gone astray,
> each of us has turned to our own way;
> and the Lord has laid on him
> the iniquity of us all.

To leave no doubt as to where I am going with this, look also at what Paul writes in 2 Corinthians 5:21: "God made him who had no sin to be sin for us, so that in him we might become the righteousness of God." So, in touching and healing the leper, Jesus deliberately took on that man's uncleanness so he could render him clean and take away his sin. Paul says that Jesus became sin for us. This cannot be more sacrilegious. Yet that exactly was the plan of God for his Son. How else could he redeem a fallen human race?

One more verse that would help drive this home is 1 John 2:2, where we read: "He is the atoning sacrifice for our sins, and not only for ours but also for the sins of the whole world."

So what we have in the story of the leper is the cross before the Cross. It is the redemption story beginning to unfold. It is the plan of God for the salvation of unclean, sinful humanity personified in this leper. It is there for us to see ourselves in the leper, and for us to allow Jesus to reach out and also touch us!

Leprosy may only be something we read of in the Bible, or in other books. But sin is not. We know it firsthand; we have seen it firsthand, and, sadly, we continue to live it firsthand. Sin is the true leprosy that will only go away with the touch of the Redeemer as we allow him to take our filth and sins on himself and clothe us in his righteousness.

We must ask one last question: Is it permissible that God incarnate would take on himself humanity's uncleanness and guilt? The answer is that it is not only permissible; it is beyond permissible. It is imperative. Our very salvation is contingent on it.

CHAPTER 10

Scriptural Contradictions
Explaining the First Commission

MATTHEW 10 AND JOHN 4

No one argues against differences in the Bible, not even the most adamant biblical conservative. Matthew 21 says that Jesus tells his followers to find a donkey with her colt so that he could enter Jerusalem on Palm Sunday, whereas John 12 speaks only of a young donkey that Jesus rides on. Was it just the colt or was its mother also there with it? This difference is easily explainable: Jesus was riding the colt, and it wasn't important to John to mention that its mother was there too.

However, other contradictory statements or positions are not as easily answered. To address them takes careful observation and more extensive investigation. One must dig a little deeper, and prayerfully continue tapping the soil of the Word.

One such case is the Lord's first commission to his disciples as it appears in Matthew 10:5–6: "These twelve Jesus sent out with the following instructions: 'Do not go among the Gentiles or enter any town of the Samaritans. Go rather to the lost sheep of Israel.'" Against that we have John's account of Jesus meeting and conversing with a Samaritan woman.

> Just then his disciples returned and were surprised to find him talking with a woman. But no one asked, "What do you want?" or "Why are you talking with her?" Then, leaving her water jar, the woman went back to the town and said to the people, "Come, see a man who told me everything I ever did. Could this be the Messiah?" They came out of the town and made their way toward him.
>
> Many of the Samaritans from that town believed in him because of the woman's testimony, "He told me everything I ever did." So when the Samaritans came to him, they urged him to stay with them, and he stayed two days. And because of his words many more became believers. (John 4:27–29, 39–41).

A reader may ask why Jesus did something completely against his orders to the Twelve. Jesus told them explicitly not to enter any town of the Samaritans, and we find him doing exactly the opposite. Not only does he enter their town, but he also stays there for two days. If that is not a contradiction, then what is it?

Let me start by pointing out a couple of things. The first is that the question is valid. Jesus could not be asking one thing and doing another. He was a man of integrity, and since we have no reason to doubt his marching orders to the Twelve in Matthew 10, and we have no reason to doubt the truthfulness of John's testimony in John 4, there must be an explanation that we will need to work harder to understand.

We also need to realize that even the disciples, when they return from their shopping trip and see Jesus at the well talking with a Samaritan woman, were puzzled and surprised. Not only was Jesus talking to a woman; he was talking to a Samaritan woman. No one asked anything. But that did not mean they weren't wondering why Jesus would do something that they were ordered not to do.

The argument that many biblical commentators and expositors suggest is that the first offer of salvation was to be made to the Jews, the lost sheep of Israel. The Gentiles or the Samaritans should not have the Gospel presented to them until the Jewish people first refuse it. To help solidify this argument, these expositors then quote John 1:11, that Jesus "came to that which was his own," meaning to the Jewish people.

But then, such a position leaves what Jesus did in John 4 unanswered. This encounter with the Samaritan woman took place early on in his ministry. He still had three years to get his people to accept him and his message. In other words, he did not wait until his people refused the Gospel before going to the Samaritans himself!

Biblical scholars also tell us that Matthew was written for a Jewish audience. We can accept that; yet, writing for a Jewish audience doesn't mean that Matthew tampered with his Gospel to please the Jews. That would be an outrageous, unfounded accusation. There must be another reasonable explanation for this ostensible contradiction.

Before offering what I believe to be a plausible answer to this dilemma, I would like for us to invite Luke as a witness in our discussion by turning to Luke 9:51–55.

> As the time approached for him to be taken up
> to heaven, Jesus resolutely set out for Jerusalem.
> And he sent messengers on ahead, who went into
> a Samaritan village to get things ready for him; but
> the people there did not welcome him, because
> he was heading for Jerusalem. When the disciples

James and John saw this, they asked, "Lord, do you want us to call fire down from heaven to destroy them?" But Jesus turned and rebuked them.

This happened toward the latter part of the ministry of our Lord on earth. Jesus was setting his eyes out for Jerusalem. This would be the last trip he would make into the city before he was judged by the Sanhedrin and by Pilate and sentenced to death.

In preparation for that, he sent messengers to see if he and his followers could go through Samaritan country. The answer was no. He was not welcome, nor were his followers.

Of special interest to us is the immediate reaction of two of the Twelve, namely the sons of thunder, James and John. The Samaritans, according to these two, merited only one thing: fire from heaven. They wanted Jesus to send total destruction and annihilation, similar to what happened to Sodom and Gomorrah!

With that attitude in the background, let us now go back to Matthew 10. Imagine for a moment Jesus commissioning his Twelve, including James and John, to go anywhere they wanted to preach the coming of the Kingdom. Imagine that Jesus did not order them to limit their ministry to the lost sheep of Israel, but to go to gentile country and to Samaritan towns and villages. And imagine that James and John headed to Samaria. I would think that with such racism and spiritual blindness, one of two things would have happened. Either this would have been the end of anything called Samaritan—since these two would have brought down fire from heaven on those towns and villages and burned them up—or it would have been the end of James and John, because some Samaritan thugs would have put an early end to them and their ministry.

What does this mean? It means that Jesus knew what he was doing. He knew the guys that he had called to follow him. He knew what their limitations were. They were Jewish bigots who would have issues with non-Jews even after the Holy Spirit came upon them on the day of Pentecost. The risks were too great. The Twelve could lose their lives. They could be met with antagonism from the Samaritans! The Samaritan people would lose a golden opportunity to know their Savior! The Samaritans could even be burned alive!

Jesus came for everyone. He did not have issues with either Samaritans or Gentiles. The Jews even accused him of being a Samaritan.

So was his action really a contradiction in positions? Obviously not! Jesus did not contradict himself. Once we get a proper understanding of the Word, we bend our knees to the Lord who continues to welcome all who will believe, regardless of race, skin color, ethnic background, or other such outward differences.

It is obvious that we still have quite some homework to do and that there is quite some work for the Holy Spirit to do in our hearts. There are probably some among us who are not even prepared to go to their own people, let alone go to the "Gentiles" or "Samaritans"! The message to us today is simple: If we cannot accept others and love them, we had better stay home. There is no point in trying to share a Gospel of love with someone we cannot or do not want to love. That would be very inconsistent.

CHAPTER 11

Sink or Swim
When a Fisherman Begins to Drown

MATTHEW 14:22–31

I grew up in the Old City of Jerusalem, and immediately before that I had lived for some years at an orphanage for boys in the little town of Bethany. My childhood did not afford me the opportunity to learn how to swim.

In the 1980s and 1990s, my family lived in southern Europe. Our apartment was 3 minutes away from the beach. Our four boys learned how to swim because that was a school requirement. Although we would often spend time as a family at the beach, in case of an emergency, neither my wife nor I could do anything except call for help.

Did I try to learn how to swim? Yes, I did. I wanted to enjoy the beach and the water. I asked one of our workmates who was a good swimmer to teach me. But as soon as my back touched the water, I was immobilized. I screamed and pleaded to get out.

Because of my fear of water, the story of Peter walking on water has always intrigued me. As the account in Matthew

14:22–31 goes, the disciples saw Jesus walking toward them on the water. They were terrified, thinking it was a ghost, but Peter got out and walked toward Jesus. At one point, he grew afraid and immediately began to sink.

By profession, Peter was a fisherman. He lived by and worked on the Sea of Galilee, which is a large lake that can get very rough with high waves. Peter was willing to face the waves head-on. For that we definitely give him credit. However, why did Peter sink? We assume that he must have been a good swimmer because he was a fisherman, but that isn't necessarily true. Fishermen in Jesus' time often did not know how to swim. This may seem odd to us, but it was often the case. If, for the sake of argument, we say that Peter was a strong swimmer, then why did he sink?

I can think of three reasons. First, Peter turned his eyes away from Jesus and began to look at and think of the wind. Even excellent swimmers can drown in rough water if they lose focus or get distracted. Likewise, anytime we turn our eyes away from Jesus we get into trouble. For example, we may allow our frustrations and constant quest for answers to consume us. Why do good people suffer? Why are innocent children born with illnesses or disabilities? Why do our prayers go unanswered? There are more "whys" than we can humanly answer. And when these questions take center stage and become the focal point of our attention, we begin to lose ground. In such cases, we must keep looking at Jesus. This will not only take our minds away from our circumstances and nagging questions, but it may also lead us to some answers. We will know, if nothing else, that suffering is not haphazard. We will see that God may well have a plan in mind when he allows suffering. We will understand that God can use suffering redemptively in the same way that he allowed his own Son to hang on a cross. To continue looking at Jesus becomes our antidote in the face of the winds of this world that would otherwise buffet us.

A second reason, according to the statement that Jesus made, was that Peter began to doubt. What doubt did Peter have? What doubt was Jesus referring to? Matthew does not go into detail. Before I answer that specific question, let me point out that Peter was always first to talk. Even in this instance, none of his friends asked to verify that the "ghost" was truly Jesus. And in this case, Peter was not confirming his allegiance to Jesus; rather, he was voicing his doubts. His question and request reflected those doubts. He said, "Lord, if it's you, tell me to come to you on the water" (Matthew 14:28). Peter was putting Jesus to the test. He should have known better than to do this. It would take time before Peter would completely trust the Master. Even after Jesus was put to the test and proved who he was, Peter continued to doubt. He was already walking on water as he went to meet Jesus. But then, doubt crept in again. Peter doubted if he could make it all the way. He could start walking toward Jesus, but would he be able to continue his journey?

A third reason for his sinking, in my estimate, was that Peter, the brave, who stood higher than his companions and ventured to go out and walk on water, needed to know his limitations. Peter, the boastful, needed to learn that he could not depend on his skills or his knowledge. Peter, the leader, had to learn that he was at least as vulnerable as any of his companions. Peter had to learn to acknowledge his weakness. The waves were stronger than he was. He had to face reality. He needed someone outside of himself to save him from drowning!

When I consider myself with regard to this incident, several questions come to mind. Are there things for me to learn here? Am I dependent on my skills, my diplomas, or my relationships for salvation? Have I discovered my constant need to look at Jesus? Do I have the faith and the courage to ask for Jesus' help before, through, and after the stormy events of life?

I also need to realize that, just like Peter, I am dependent on Jesus to come to my rescue when my faith fails me. When my faith is only able to carry me so far on the world's stormy seas, I want his hand to also reach out to me and catch me. Without his reaching to me, I know I will drown. Doubts that creep in are enough to drown me. Alone, I cannot make it. I always need Jesus to meet me halfway! I am safe only in his hands.

CHAPTER 12

The Coins of God
Bible Verses Out of Context

MATTHEW 22:15–21

I find it quite intriguing when the world borrows verses and stories from Scripture and uses them to fit a specific agenda, be it political, social, or cultural. The more ironic element for me in this context is that, in many cases, only part of a verse is quoted to corroborate a certain leaning, perspective, or interpretation. When people do that, they run the risk of losing the fuller picture. If it is critical to look at the verses that precede and follow a certain verse, then , it is even more essential to study an individual verse in its entirety. Halving the verse can completely undermine its meaning and message.

Matthew 22:21 is one verse that is often sliced in the middle. The first half—"Give back to Caesar what is Caesar's" —is quoted mostly by those who stress civic duty. It is as if Caesar—meaning government in all its forms and levels—is the essence of the answer Jesus gave when asked if it was right to pay the imperial tax to Caesar.

Before we go any further, remember that the issue of taxation was huge for Jesus' audience. Israel was occupied by the Romans, who imposed heavy taxes. As Matthew points out in verse 15, the Pharisees were plotting to trap Jesus. This would be neither their first nor their last attempt. They made taxes and money their bait this time, hoping to outsmart Jesus. At other times they would use other types of bait. In this case, if Jesus were to side with the Pharisees against taxation, he would be accused of rebellion against Rome. Herodians—agents of the Roman authorities— were also in the audience. If Jesus were to side with the Herodians and be pro-tax, then the Pharisees, the Zealots, and other people hoping for liberation from the Romans would turn against him. But Jesus was ready for them, saying "Give back to Caesar what is Caesar's, and to God what is God's" (Matthew 22:21).

The new dimension that Jesus brings into the discussion, the second half of the verse, had not surfaced in the mind or conscience of either group. God, and what could potentially belong to God, were not on their agenda at all. Even money per se was not the issue here.

Faced with their question, Jesus asked that they show him a Roman coin. He knew what Roman coins looked like because he was living under the same occupation. Even the temple tax was paid in Roman coins. Jesus asked to have the coin not for him to learn, but for his adversaries to have a better look at it. In fact, Jesus has another, much more important coin in mind. To introduce that more important coin, he asked whose image and inscription were on the Roman coin.

This question took the two groups by surprise, not because it was strange, but because its answer was too obvious. They knew as well as he did whose image and inscription were on the coin. Nonetheless, they answer him: the image and inscription are Caesar's. To their utter amazement and shock, Jesus then gives his profound answer: "So give back to Caesar what is Caesar's, and to God what is God's" (Matthew 22:21).

Jesus was not a rebel who had come to rouse his people against the occupation. Nor was he a liberation theologian. As a good citizen, like his compatriots, when the time came to pay one's taxes, he would do that. He was above reproach in every sense.

But that is only one side of the coin. That was the human side of things, the first half of his profound answer.

Jesus used the coin as a preamble to a much bigger and more important matter. Then, as now, many governments want everything, not just one's money. In many cases, they even want to own the individual, robbing him or her of rights, privileges, freedom, and even his or her soul. Jesus clearly states that there are things that you owe to the government, but you do not owe everything. And so he said, "(give) to God what is God's."

But what is God's? Was Jesus speaking of the temple tax? Was he talking of paying one's tithes or offerings? Was he talking of money in general?

Jesus would have none of that. Money is not his issue. Money is for people and governments. God owns everything. He does not want or need our money. He is the one who gave it to us in the first place, so why would he be after it? We might think we please him when we pay out tithes and offerings, but that is a very ludicrous idea.

So, I ask again: What is God's? The answer is in the question that Jesus asked. His question was whose image and inscription were on the coin. Based on the answer he got, he said to give to Caesar what belongs to Caesar; namely, the money that bears his image. In the same way, that which bears God's image belongs to God. And who bears the image of the Creator? We do. We are God's coins! Genesis 1:27 presents this fascinating truth: "So God created mankind in his own image, in the image of God he created them; male and female he created them."

What is the bottom line? We belong to God. As a matter of fact, we belong to him not once, but twice. First, we bear his image. Second, when we sinned and went astray and his image was disfigured in us, he brought us back to himself in Christ and put his Spirit in us. Our mind, heart, body, emotions, reason, time, money, and everything else about us belongs to him. How much of us does he own? The better question may be: How much of us does he control?

CHAPTER 13

The Power to Heal
Why Did Jesus Touch the Blind Man Twice?

MARK 8:22–26

Some Bible passages invite the reader to investigate and discover why an event does not fully make sense to him or to her. In other passages, the author does not leave room for such personal effort. One example of the latter is in Matthew 13:58. The author clearly states that in his hometown, Jesus "did not do many miracles there because of their lack of faith."

Mark 6:5 offers a little more information: "[Jesus]could not do any miracles there, except lay his hands on a few sick people and heal them." In verse 6, Mark goes on to say that Jesus "was amazed at their lack of faith." Both Matthew and Mark agree that the people's lack of faith was the hurdle that stood in the way of Jesus performing miracles. From these accounts, we can be certain that lack of faith ties the hands of Jesus. By extrapolation, the opposite should therefore be true: faith should move the hands of Jesus. But then we come up against Mark 8:22–26:

They came to Bethsaida, and some people brought a blind man and begged Jesus to touch him. He took the blind man by the hand and led him outside the village. When he had spit on the man's eyes and put his hands on him, Jesus asked, "Do you see anything?"

He looked up and said, "I see people; they look like trees walking around."

Once more Jesus put his hands on the man's eyes. Then his eyes were opened, his sight was restored, and he saw everything clearly. Jesus sent him home, saying, "Don't even go into the village."

Jesus had to touch the blind man not once but twice for him to regain his full sight. What is going on? Normally one single touch from Jesus was enough to heal blindness, leprosy, or any other disease. We have other events in which people simply touched his clothes and received immediate healing. What's going on? Has the power of Jesus diminished over time?

Three things stand out in the text. The first is the hometown of this man: Bethsaida. This was one of two towns in the Galilee in which Jesus had performed a good number of miracles. Yet unlike other towns, no one from Bethsaida seems to have repented. That was the reason behind the dire warning and the judgment that Jesus had pronounced on it: "Woe to you, Bethsaida! For, if the miracles that were performed in you had been performed in Tyre and Sidon, they would have repented long ago in sackcloth and ashes" (Matthew 11:21).

In this verse, Jesus is saying that miracles were not meant to be an end in themselves. Rather, when the Lord intervenes with a miracle, there is always a higher purpose. In every case, miracles display his power and his glory. Miracles can also lead a person to faith and repentance. Seemingly, Bethsaida only opted for the miracle. The ministry of Jesus did not bear much fruit in that town. If anything, the townspeople were inviting more judgment. More divine intervention plus less human response always equals more judgment!

The second important observation is that Jesus took the blind man by his hand and led him outside the village. That was a first. This is the only time we read of Jesus having to lead someone away from the neighbors and the town before healing the person. Jesus testified that he had performed many miracles in Bethsaida. So why not one more? Was Jesus seeking to save that town from harsher judgment for failing to repent? Or was he unwilling to give them another chance to witness a miracle and repent?

These are open questions for which we can only theorize. I am personally of the opinion that there is a time for everything. There is a time for grace, and there is a time when God stops knocking on the door of someone's life. It was not Jesus who shut the door of grace. Bethsaida did. Jesus respected their decision. There was no further need to forcefully open their hearts to the truth.

The third observation is that Jesus sent the man back to his home yet warned him not to go into the village. In some manuscripts, Jesus even instructs the man not to tell anyone in the village. This was so unlike Jesus. Not that he was always asking for publicity, but on at least a few other occasions, Jesus told the person he had healed to talk about the healing. One classic example is in Luke 8:39, in which Jesus told the Gerasene demoniac to "return home and tell how much God has done for you." Luke adds that "the man went away and told all over town how much Jesus had done for him."

Apparently, this case is different because Bethsaida is different. Jesus knew it would be futile to witness to a group of people who would not believe or repent anyway. In addition, Jesus may have realized that the townspeople could also physically, emotionally, or spiritually attack this man. Jesus had planted a new seed into a new heart with the hope that someday this seed might bear fruit. It would surely make more sense to keep the person away from unrepentant and unbelieving people. The exhortation that Jesus gave in Matthew 7:6 would perfectly apply in this situation: "Do not give dogs what is sacred; do not throw your pearls to pigs. If you do, they may trample them under their feet, and turn and tear you to pieces."

But let us return to the original question: Why did Jesus have to touch the man twice? Perhaps the man's faith just wasn't strong enough. Just imagine for a moment what would have happened if Jesus had left the man only seeing partially. He would be in a more miserable situation than he was when he was completely blind. At least then, people may have had pity on him as he begged. But now, everyone would think he could see clearly when in fact, he could not. That would have been a curse rather than a blessing. Jesus touched him twice so that both his sight and his faith would be complete.

My first reflection on all this is somewhat personal. As I reflect on the number of times that Jesus has had to touch me personally and to open my eyes to the truth about him, about life, and even about myself, I stand indebted and thankful that he did not do that only once, or even only twice. The numbers are too many to count. It is not because his touches were incomplete. It is because of my shortsightedness, stubbornness, and sinfulness that I need to be touched again and again.

My second reflection is to remember that faith is not for everyone. For inasmuch as God may want everyone to be saved and inasmuch as we want to see people accept the truth and be saved, some will never believe. They have sealed their own destiny. Even miracles will not change their minds or turn their hearts toward God. Sadly, they are no better than the inhabitants of Bethsaida. The seeds that are sown will bear fruit in some people but not in others. If we doubt that, we need only look at the life of the Master himself.

CHAPTER 14

In a Manger
Does It Matter Where Jesus Was Born?

LUKE 2:1-12

Ever since my childhood days, I have always been fascinated by the Christmas story. I loved watching the Sisters of Charity in Bethany work hours to build a crèche for the Holy Family. Their preparations would build up to a sort of crescendo on the night of December 24, and then I would look forward to a delicious cup of hot chocolate and a sugar bun the next day. To a young orphan boy my age, it was surreal.

On Christmas day, priests would flock to our orphanage, some robed in white and others robed in black or other colors. They would take the platform in our small church building and tell again and again the story of the little baby boy born in a manger to poor parents in the small town of Bethlehem.

At the time, the explanation of those good priests made sense. Jesus was born in a manger not only because his parents were poor and not only because there was no room for them in the inn. He was born there to identify with the poor and humble. Such a message could not have been more appropriate to poor boys living at an orphanage. It resonated with us. We were poor, but Jesus was even poorer, and he identified himself with us.

In my late teens, I received my first pocket copy of the New Testament, since the Second Vatican Council had made it possible for Catholics to have greater access to the Scriptures. To say that the Christmas story was the first thing I looked up that day would be an exaggeration. I didn't. But over time, and with repeated readings of the New Testament, the issue of the birth of Jesus in a manger resurfaced in my inquisitive mind.

Why the manger? Mary and Joseph were not the only poor couple at the time. Why don't we hear of other poor Jewish babies being born in mangers?

In considering the broader context of Jesus' birth—the events and circumstances that surrounded it—another question surfaced. Why were the shepherds the very first group to get the news?

One potential answer is that those shepherds happened to be nearby, so the angels did not have to go very far. They could get the good news out faster! Or, maybe with the shepherds being so close, the Holy Family would not have to wait long before receiving the first congratulations. It would be mere minutes before the shepherds would be at their "door."

Let's not beat around the bush and avoid the one question that ought to be asked at the very start: Why a manger?

We need to ask what mangers were used for. What purpose did they serve? Or to put it more succinctly, who or what would be laid in a manger when born? With such pertinent questions, we begin to see the true image and meaning more clearly. Mangers were never meant for babies; rather, they were meant for little lambs. This is where a shepherd might put a newborn lamb that needed a little extra attention. A manger was a safe and protected place.

So why was Jesus placed in a manger? You guessed it. Because this is where lambs were placed, and since he was the Lamb of God, it is quite understandable that he would begin his life in a manger. In addition, lambs that were to be used in Temple sacrifice were sometimes placed in mangers in order to examine them for blemishes. The manger, then, became the place where the perfect lambs were discovered. And Jesus is the most perfect "lamb" of all—the Lamb of God.

This obviously answers the question of the manger, but why were the shepherds the first to receive the good news? It had nothing to do with them being close by. No, the fact is that if ever there were a group of people who would celebrate the birth of a new lamb to their flock, it would be the shepherds. It all fits. Oh, the wisdom of God has been hidden from the wise and haughty and given to the unwise of this world.

This also ties in neatly and perfectly with the lambs that the Israelites in Egypt had to slaughter in order to use their blood on the sides and tops of their doorframes so that the Angel of Death would pass over them. This is the true Passover story retold in a manger in the town of Bethlehem. It is the story of the crucified lamb who is photo-framed in a manger.

The image of Jesus as the Lamb also fits perfectly well with how he is revealed to John in the Book of Revelation. The term "Lamb" appears no less than thirty-one times in that one book alone.

The wisdom of God is so amazing! His love for us is also so amazing. He had planned our salvation and redemption and a means of reconciliation even before the creation of the world. Yet we only began to get a glimpse of it in the little baby boy wrapped in a cloth and laid in a manger! How marvelous and glorious that first Christmas morning was, and how uniquely blessed were those shepherds!

CHAPTER 15

Divine Appointments
Letting God Control Our Schedules

LUKE 8:40–50

I f anyone is a slave to time, I am. If, for whatever reason, I am late for an appointment, my blood pressure goes up. I strive to be early for every appointment I have. During the time my family and I lived in Kenya, Africa, in the late 1970s, I heard many times the expression, "You have a watch, but we have the time."

As I've grown older, and hopefully a little wiser, I realize that although time, schedules, and appointments should be respected, they must not be our masters. We need the grace to allow God to interrupt all that for his higher and nobler purposes. Let me tell you a little story to illustrate this point.

My flight from Erbil, Kurdistan, landed at about 9:40 pm at Istanbul's Ataturk airport. My next flight was scheduled for 6:00 am. The layover would give me a few hours of sleep at the airport hotel. All I had to do was make my way to a transfer desk, go through security, go up two flights of stairs or take an elevator, and walk across the terminal to the hotel. All in all, I figured it would be a simple 15- or 20-minute walk and then I could go to bed. I did not even consider having a late dinner, even though I had not had much to eat that afternoon or evening. As I went to passport entry, I was glad I had made the decision to book my hotel on site. Thousands of passengers were standing in long lines waiting for their passports to be stamped. I looked at my watch. It was 9:50 pm.

Several lines were open, and a good number of security agents were managing the screening process. Within seconds my carry-on bag, belt, and watch were on the conveyor belt. I was about to take my shoes off when a huge explosion rattled the building. I could see particles floating in the air around me, but I couldn't smell anything. One second my things were on the moving belt, the next second, all the security agents, as well as the thousands of arriving passengers, started screaming and running. The police officers were urging people to run as fast as they could.

I picked up my carry-on, watch, and belt, walked back a few feet, and stood still. I knew something was going on, but I didn't know what. There was not a soul in sight but me, but I was at peace. Fifteen minutes later, passengers started filling up the immigration lines again, but no one was managing the booths. With the absence of any information from the airport's PA system, nobody knew what was going on. I was glad that I had not left my spot. I told myself that once the security agents came back, I would be the first to go through.

But just a few minutes later, I heard a second explosion, not as loud as the first. Once again, arriving passengers started running and falling on top of each other, with many screaming at the top of their voices. Once again, I just stood there. People must have thought that I was either completely deaf or completely dumb or both. Ten minutes later, passengers once again began lining up.

For two long hours I remained standing, waiting, and hoping. I did not really care what was going on. I just wanted to sleep, but there was no way I could get to the hotel. There was no internet connection, no information at the airport, and no news from the outside world. Finally, I gave up and found a seat. We were not going anywhere anytime soon. By then, the airport was filling up with passengers from more flights. Without anyone permitted to leave the arrival hall, people could not find a place to sit or even stand.

Another hour passed. It was now past 1:00 am. Sitting next to me were three Arabs, one from Palestine, one from Jordan, and one from Algeria. With time on our hands and nothing much to do, and following a good Arab custom, we spent the next three hours visiting. In the meantime, with an internet connection restored, I got one message from the airline saying that my flight to Paris was canceled. More messages came from friends saying that this was a terrorist attack by ISIS and that more terrorists were hiding at the airport. That obviously explained our lockdown.

I happened to be the only Christian among the small group of Arabs. We dove into politics, a subject matter close to the heart of Arabs. But, now that we all knew who was behind these attacks, I thought that it was my chance to begin explaining the Gospel message.

I wish I could say that all three men believed in and accepted Christ into their lives that eventful night and dawn. They didn't. But by the end, they knew they were sinners in need of a savior. They knew that Islam, as it was being shown to the world by ISIS, was not the answer. They heard me explain why Jesus had to die. They were my captive audience. They could not even leave their seats without risking losing them to other passengers wanting to sit down. Around 4:00 pm, the airport was finally reopened and we were all cleared to go on our way—I to my hotel and my companions to immigration. One of the three told me that when he gets back home to Jordan, he would purchase a copy of the New Testament.

Looking back today, I ask myself, "Was it worth it all?" A suicide bomber had blown himself up some 50 feet away from where I was standing. My flight was canceled. On top of it all, I discovered that the hotel was not accepting any more guests because of the attack, so I spent the rest of that sleepless night on a bench in the departure hall. Was it worth it? The short answer is a definite yes. There were three souls there who needed to hear the Gospel, and God honored me to be his witness that eventful night. If that was not a divine appointment, I do not know what it was!

My slavery to time and to my watch has everything to do with me and my image. More often than not, it has nothing to do with God's plan and purpose, whether for someone else or for me. At times like these, what I need is to gladly surrender my time, and give my plans and my life away to God. He may have my name on his schedule, for another such divine appointment! And since he controls his schedule and I don't, I want to be open and willing to have my schedule disrupted and interrupted at any time. As we read in Luke 8:40–50, even Jesus allowed his schedule to be interrupted by the Father's plans!

CHAPTER 16

The Good Samaritan
The True Message of the Parable

LUKE 10:25–37

Before we dig into the Parable of the Good Samaritan as it appears in Luke 10:25–37, let us read it carefully with the hope of really understanding the message Jesus intended to convey through it.

On one occasion an expert in the law stood up to test Jesus. "Teacher," he asked, "what must I do to inherit eternal life?"

"What is written in the Law?" he replied. "How do you read it?"

He answered, "'Love the Lord your God with all your heart and with all your soul and with all your strength and with all your mind'; and, 'Love your neighbor as yourself.'"

"You have answered correctly," Jesus replied. "Do this and you will live."

But he wanted to justify himself, so he asked Jesus, "And who is my neighbor?"

In reply Jesus said: "A man was going down from Jerusalem to Jericho, when he was attacked by robbers. They stripped him of his clothes, beat him and went away, leaving him half dead. A priest happened to be going down the same road, and when he saw the man, he passed by on the other side. So too, a Levite, when he came to the place and saw him, passed by on the other side. But a Samaritan, as he traveled, came where the man was; and when he saw him, he took pity on him. He went to him and bandaged his wounds, pouring on oil and wine. Then he put the man on his own donkey, brought him to an inn and took care of him. The next day he took out two denarii and gave them to the innkeeper. 'Look after him,' he said, 'and when I return, I will reimburse you for any extra expense you may have.'

"Which of these three do you think was a neighbor to the man who fell into the hands of robbers?"

The expert in the Law replied, "The one who had mercy on him."

Jesus told him, "Go and do likewise."

Two questions found in this passage give us the key to properly understanding the message that Jesus was conveying to this expert of the Law. The first is, "Who is my neighbor?" The second is, "Which of these three . . . was a neighbor to the man?"

The first is asked by the expert of the Law. On the surface, there is nothing out of the ordinary about his rather straightforward question. He knows who God is, and so he can choose to love him. But, he is asking for someone to explain and identify who his neighbor is, so that he can choose to love him, too.

Yet as we explore this man's question, we can see that it harbors a passive attitude that speaks of someone who will only react rather than act. The expert of the Law would consider loving someone else, but only after that person becomes a neighbor to him. It goes without saying that this is not about someone living next door to one's house, but, rather, a more generalized sense of the word "neighbor."

Did you notice that Jesus does not answer the man's specific question? In his answer, Jesus shows a world of difference between someone who, like this expert of the Law, is passive and will only react, and someone who, against the odds, takes the first step.

Jesus' answer turns the table downside up. Rather than wait until a neighbor has been identified and then acting in love, Jesus presents the man with a perfect example of how loving a neighbor is translated into actual life. Jesus' dramatic and colorful parable was not foreign to this man's history or culture. It left no excuses for misunderstanding or second guesses.

The man going on the journey from Jerusalem to Jericho was obviously a Jew. Jerusalem was the Jewish capital city. The priest and the Levite were also Jews. Yet despite their religious and ethnic affinity with their injured compatriot, they turned their faces and eyes away from him. But that element is not the crux of the parable. Jesus was not speaking against either the priest or the Levite, as some Scripture expositors would have us believe. So, what is the punch line of the parable?

The punch line starts with the appearance of the Samaritan, someone whom the Jews considered to be an enemy and an apostate. The Jews would not allow the Samaritans to sacrifice in the Temple at Jerusalem and considered marriages between Samaritans and Jews to be illegal.

From the Samaritan perspective, the Judaism brought back by those who returned after the captivity in Babylon had been changed and corrupted. The Samaritans worshipped at Mount Gerizim, not the Jerusalem Temple. Hatred between the two groups was reciprocal.

To the ears of the expert of the Law, the Samaritan has no place in this parable. The mere mention of the word probably made him shiver. For while neither priest nor Levite tended to the needs of the man by the road, the enemy, the outcast, did.

The Jewish man by the roadside is not the Samaritan's compatriot. Yet when he saw this Jewish man naked, injured, and lying by the roadside, the Samaritan went out of his way to help him. The Samaritan chose to become a neighbor to the Jew. If he were to wait for that Jew to first become his neighbor before showering him with his acts of kindness, he would be waiting to this day.

The Samaritan became the hero of the parable because he took the initiative and made the first step. The Jewish man was not his religious neighbor since they worshipped at different places and had different beliefs. Nor was the Jewish man his ethnic neighbor, since one was considered pure and the other of mixed-race. Finally, the Jewish man was not even his geographical neighbor, since one lived in Judea and one lived in Samaria. In spite of all these differences, he built a bridge of neighborliness by taking the initiative to go toward this fellow and take care of him. He saw a fellow human being in need and reached out to him. That, in essence, is what it means to love one's neighbor.

Ethnic, religious, cultural, and geographical differences will blind us to the needs of others, so that we do not reach out to them. In contrast, love can help us to look past these differences so that we can reach out to others in love and service.

Jesus ends his discussion with the expert of the Law by admonishing him to "go and do likewise." Go and become a neighbor. Do not hold your love back until someone else takes the first step. Rather, you take the first step. The expert of the Law asked who his neighbor was, but Jesus was not interested in answering a passive question and attitude like that. Jesus' answer places the responsibility on all of us to actively seek to become neighbors to anyone and everyone, even our enemies!

How much of a better place the world would be today if we were to follow that simple principle. Not only would individuals establish more neighborly relationships, but ethnic differences would also begin to dissipate, religious differences would stop causing conflicts and atrocities, and countries would be less likely to be at war with each other. The world would be a better place for everyone. Everyone, regardless of race, ethnicity, religious background, skin color, culture, or any other factor is a potential neighbor. Let us take the initiative and become a neighbor!

CHAPTER 17

Drawing Conclusions
What Are Certain Parables Really About?

LUKE 15

Can we entertain the notion that there are misleading statements in the Bible? I am not talking here about what is known in some circles as higher criticism. I am talking of a Bible student like myself discovering titles that are not quite correct. Is that even possible?

Before being accused of heresy, allow me to explain. In many Bibles, publishers have taken the liberty of adding what they believe to be the main message of a specific paragraph. For a simple Bible student, the additional verbiage added by these publishers can be misunderstood to be part and parcel of the Word of God; worse, it is also often accepted as the true interpretation of the passage.

I personally have two problems with this. The first problem is that it takes away the personal investigation and careful study that each of us should be doing on our own. We are being spoon-fed, and that is not permissible. The second, much more serious problem, is that at times these publishers get it wrong, pure and simple. They miss the mark altogether. The reader is left with something the text does not even attempt to teach. It is in light of this fact that I asked above if we can entertain the notion that some statements in the Bible could be misleading.

Now that we know the background, the answer is sadly, yes. I did not and do not mean that these publishers got it wrong every time, or that every little title they invented was off track. But quite a few are, and the general observation that Bible students should be allowed to study the Word completely independently and without interference stands.

Take Luke 15. One well-known Bible gives titles to what the publisher perceives to be the three main parts of this chapter. Those titles are: Parable of the Lost Sheep, Parable of the Lost Coin, and Parable of the Lost Son. I can almost hear someone murmuring that there is nothing wrong with those three titles. Each title seems to be summing up the main subject matter of the section that it covers. Yes, each title seems to, but does it really sum up the main subject matter? Why did I underline the word *main*? Because this is what titles are supposed to do. They are supposed to sum up in very concise form the main idea or thought for the section or paragraph that follows. And in this case, I think the publisher missed the mark completely.

The key to correctly understanding any text necessitates looking at context; that is, what surrounds the specific text. This is true not only of the Bible, but also of any book, newspaper article, and so on. We often hear the statement that such and such was taken out of context, either of what was written or what was said. If making such accusations of general speech is serious, then how much more serious when we neglect to look for the context of specific passages in the Word of God?

There are three types of contexts that we should pay attention to. The first is the immediate context; that is, the words or phrases immediately preceding or following a given text. Next is the intermediate context, which refers to the preceding or following chapter or chapters. It can also refer to the totality of the book or Gospel in question. Last is the distant context, which refers to the Bible in its totality. The bottom line is that for a given text to be correctly understood, it would have to be compatible and in agreement with its immediate context, its intermediate context, and the overarching message of the Bible.

Now back to Luke 15. We will content ourselves with looking at the immediate context to see the circumstances in which Jesus told these three parables and how those circumstances can aid our understanding.

Verses 1 and 2 read as follows: "Now the tax collectors and sinners were all gathering around to hear Jesus. But the Pharisees and the teachers of the law muttered, 'This man welcomes sinners and eats with them.'"

These two verses give us the immediate context, the circumstances that led Jesus to tell his parables. They are our main resource to correctly understand the message or messages that Jesus intended to teach. If we bypass these two verses and jump directly to the paragraphs that follow, chances are we will miss the main messages contained therein, and thus our titles will be off the mark. These verses speak of two things. The first is that Jesus welcomed tax collectors and sinners into his fellowship. He allowed them to associate with him.

The second important element is the murmuring of the Pharisees and the teachers of the Law against Jesus. They were insinuating that if Jesus were from God, he would not keep such bad company.

Luke uses an important adverb to connect verses one and two with what will follow—the word *then*. "Then Jesus told them this parable" (Luke 15:3). Luke's choice of this adverb leaves no doubt in the mind of the hearer or reader that the parables Jesus is about to present will directly respond to the accusation that he associates with sinful people.

As we read the first parable, we must ask, in what way was Jesus responding to the accusation? There is only one correct answer to this question. Jesus was basically saying that, in the same way that a shepherd would leave everything behind and spend his time looking for a lost sheep, so he is doing. He is seeking the lost sheep of Israel, those that have been lost to sin.

To make sure his hearers understand the message, Jesus goes on to present another parable, that of a woman who sweeps her house until she finds a lost coin. And once again, to bring the message even closer to home, Jesus tells the story of a father who cannot wait to see his son come back home.

Who is the main character in each of these three parables? If it were the sheep, then it would be normal and acceptable to make the sheep the central theme of the title as well. But it is not. The main message of the story is the shepherd and his love for his sheep. The same is true for the second parable. Its main message is the woman and how much she values her precious lost coin. And there is no doubt that the father and his longing to see his son come back is the main theme and message of the third story.

Based on the above, what would proper titles look like that put forward the central character and offer the main theme? These would look something like this: the parable of a shepherd's love for his sheep; the parable of a woman's esteem for her coin, and the parable of a father's longing for his son.

By placing misleading titles for these parables in Luke 15, the publishers have not only emphasized the wrong characters, but also, and more importantly, they have shifted emphasis away from the character that Jesus meant to bring to light, namely God. The shepherd, the woman, and the father all represent Jesus and God as they seek humanity in our lostness. We cannot, therefore, allow ourselves the freedom to steal the limelight from Jesus or God and put it on humanity. God is central, not humanity. God is the one looking for us and not vice versa. That search began thousands of years ago in the Garden of Eden and continues to this day. God's love for the lost is what drives these parables and that should always be the central theme: nothing more and nothing less!

Finally, I do not entertain the notion that there are misleading statements in the Bible. What I do entertain is the fact that publishers have, at times, misconstrued a passage and embedded their thoughts in the Holy Writ. Such vain attempts should stop, so that the Word of God may speak for itself. The Holy Spirit is alive and well and continues to communicate with us to this day. Human intervention can often complicate the message rather than simplify it. We have a Living God, and we have a Living Word. That Word always speaks truth. That Word always renders glory to the One to whom glory is due. The Word of God is theocentric not anthropocentric. We should view it and interpret it that way if we are to have a proper and correct understanding of it.

CHAPTER 18

Money, Money
Jesus and Financial Advice

LUKE 16:1–15

Why would Jesus talk about money and the love of money to people who did not have money? One potential reason is that although that group of people may not have had money, they may still have loved money or coveted it. Another potential reason is that although that group of people may not have had money at the time, they may have money in the future and develop love for it.

The two potential reasons above could apply to almost anyone whom Jesus was addressing during his years of ministry. But they are not too convincing if we think of the disciples. According to Matthew 27:55 and Luke 8:1–3, they were being supported by rich women. Did the Twelve have the love of money in their hearts? Could it be that while talking to his disciples, Jesus had another group in mind?

These and other questions face the serious Bible student as he or she begins to look at Luke 16:1–15, the story of the manager of a rich man who called in his master's debtors and reduced their debts. I encourage you to read the entire text for yourself.

One of the very first questions that a serious Bible student may have after reading this passage could well be the following: If Jesus was trying to teach his disciples a biblical truth, as he always did when using parables, what truth was he teaching here?

It is obvious that Jesus was not asking the Twelve to take the shrewd manager as a role model. This guy was a thief and a wheeler-dealer. He was disloyal and egoistic. So why would Jesus even bring this man's story up to the Twelve? As Jesus himself says, the manager acted shrewdly, but not ethically. This is why Jesus identified him as being of the "people of this world."

To me, Luke 16 is one of the more difficult texts in Scripture to properly understand and interpret. If Jesus were indeed addressing the Twelve, it becomes almost irrelevant for him to say to them: "I tell you, use worldly wealth to gain friends for yourselves, so that when it is gone, you will be welcomed into eternal dwellings" (Luke 16:9). Jesus knew firsthand that those guys did not have worldly wealth. As importantly, how could sharing one's wealth earn one eternal dwellings?

Moreover, verses 10 to 12 could not possibly apply to the Twelve: "Whoever can be trusted with very little can also be trusted with much, and whoever is dishonest with very little will also be dishonest with much. So if you have not been trustworthy in handling worldly wealth, who will trust you with true riches? And if you have not been trustworthy with someone else's property, who will give you property of your own?"

The Twelve were never accused of dishonesty. They had not been entrusted with someone else's property. They were not serving two masters. There is nothing in Scripture that would warrant such a warning to the Twelve.

This leads us to reconsider who it was that Jesus was really addressing. There was among them a guy named Judas Iscariot who coveted money and was stealing the coffer. (See John 12:6.) So was Jesus indirectly addressing Judas? Even that would not make much sense. According to Matthew 26:24, Jesus said: "But woe to that man who betrays the Son of Man! It would be better for him if he had not been born." Judas was not going to be welcomed into eternal dwellings regardless of what he did or did not do with worldly wealth.

The only other people listening in were the Pharisees. Is this the group that Jesus had in mind from the beginning? If Jesus had the Pharisees in mind—and this would not have been the first or last time he would confront them—then my conviction is that there was a more subtle message that Jesus was passing on to them besides the matter of money. After all, Jesus was never in the money business to begin with. He did discuss it to some degree, yet it was never at the forefront of his ministry. So why discuss it now? And why use the example of a shrewd rascal of a manager as a focal point of his parable?

Let us see if any of the verses could apply to the Pharisees, and if so, in what way or ways. The first verse in this passage introduces us to a "rich man." We ask, therefore, who did Jesus have in mind when he spoke of this "rich man"? The answer to that question depends on how we understand the parable, especially what message Jesus was trying to teach and to whom. In other parables, Jesus did not use the specific term "rich man" to refer to God. However, he did refer to a "master," such as in the parable of the "man going on a journey" found in Matthew 25:14–30. That man entrusted his servants with bags of gold. The term "master" was used seven times in that parable in a clear reference to God. The same term "master" is used to describe the rich man in the Luke 16 parable. This leaves some room to suggest that Jesus had God in mind when he referred to this "rich man."

Based on that assumption, we can now begin to draw a more comprehensive picture of this parable and how to understand and interpret it. Following this line of thinking, the parable would be an image of God who entrusted the Jewish nation with the Law, represented here by the Pharisees whose main emphasis was the keeping of that Law. Regretfully, the nation was not faithful to the spirit of the Law. If there was one group from within the Jewish nation whom Jesus constantly confronted, rebuked, and accused of dishonesty and other ills, it would be the Pharisees. This group had shrewdly taken over the management of the nation. They became the spokespeople of that nation, and, in the process, they robbed God of his rights and misled their fellow citizens.

The Pharisees were the shrewd manager. They were the stewards responsible for the care of Israel. Yet sadly, like the shrewd manager, they wasted the goods of their Master, represented in the Law of Moses. As a result, Jesus pronounced this harsh judgment against them. He could not trust them with the "true riches"; that is, the Gospel message. They had been dishonest with the Law, represented by the term "worldly wealth," which he also identified as someone else's property, meaning the property of Moses. How could Jesus give them "ownership of the Gospel message"; that is, "property of [their] own"?

The Lord did not mince his words when he talked to the Pharisees or about them. Take just one example in Matthew 16:6, 12: "Be on your guard against the yeast of the Pharisees and Sadducees. ... Then they understood that he was not telling them to guard against the yeast used in bread, but against the teaching of the Pharisees and Sadducees." Luke 16 has the same type of message, but using symbolism.

On the surface, the parable of the shrewd manager looks like it is all about money, but it is not. What Jesus is asking is this: How could the Pharisees who were not honest with someone else's property—meaning the Law of Moses—be entrusted with the message of grace? To Jesus, the Law was like worldly wealth that they had mishandled, while the message of grace was true riches.

I know that we have always taken the words of Jesus "you cannot serve both God and money" (Matthew 16:13) literally. There is no problem with such an understanding or application. It still rings true. But in this immediate context, with the Pharisees in mind, it bears a second subtle meaning. Jesus is talking about the mammon of falsehood and not just money as we know it. In that Jesus was very clear. One cannot serve God while explaining away his Word, which the Pharisees were doing.

There is still one major difficulty with one single verse, namely verse 9: "I tell you, use worldly wealth to gain friends for yourselves, so that when it is gone, you will be welcomed into eternal dwellings." Once again, I need to point out my conviction that the Lord was not addressing the Twelve but rather the Pharisees. Yet, even if my observation is correct in that Jesus was indirectly addressing the Pharisees, was he saying that they could earn eternal dwellings by sharing their worldly wealth with others? Such an interpretation would be an insult to the scores of Bible references that teach that salvation or admission to the eternal dwellings cannot be earned by anything humanity does. Rather, it is granted by the grace of God based on our Lord's work of redemption. Such an interpretation would be an insult to God and to Christ. It would make the work of redemption meaningless and needless.

So, what is the Lord saying here? If the parable was about the Pharisees, and if there was a subtle message behind using mammon, then the way to understand this would be an invitation from the Lord to the Pharisees to repent of their ways. Jesus was not closing the door on the Pharisees. Jesus was not tossing the Law aside. He said that he did not come to abolish the Law or the Prophets but to fulfill them.

So, rather than continue dealing dishonestly with the Law of Moses as was their custom, Jesus was inviting the Pharisees to repent, meaning to turn away from their ways. There was such a long list of wrongs that the Pharisees were committing and which the Lord dealt with during his ministry. This was an invitation to repent of all those. One proof of their repentance would be to begin sharing their worldly wealth with others rather than taking advantage of them. In such a case, God's dwelling would be open to them. They would be welcomed to the eternal dwellings.

Although on the surface we do not hear Jesus speak of deep theological issues, nor do we hear him speak openly about the Pharisees' need to repent, there is another occasion in the Gospels in which money was at the root of someone's problem. The person I have in mind is Zacchaeus. In Luke 19, we are told that Jesus went into the home of Zacchaeus. Soon after he did, Zacchaeus admitted his shortcomings and promised to make things right for those he had wronged. Jesus did not provoke Zacchaeus into doing what he did. To his admission, Jesus responded: "Today salvation has come to this house, because this man, too, is a son of Abraham. For the Son of Man came to seek and to save the lost" (Luke 19:9–10). In the same way, Jesus was also offering the Pharisees a way of salvation through repentance with his exhortation: "I tell you, use worldly wealth to gain friends for yourselves, so that when it is gone, you will be welcomed into eternal dwellings" (Luke 16:9).

I cannot close this excavation without referring to the fact that the Pharisees knew well that Jesus was speaking about them and against them. This is why Luke states, in verse 14, that upon hearing what Jesus had said they were sneering. It was obvious they did not like it, and soon after, they would begin plotting how they might kill him. There is one more important point to make. Notice with me the response that Jesus gives when the Pharisees sneer at him. He says to them: "You are the ones who justify yourselves in the eyes of others, but God knows your hearts" (Luke 16:15).

This verse ties things very nicely together and, for me, drives the assumption that all along Jesus had the Pharisees on his mind as he was telling the parable of the shrewd manager. In essence, he was saying that in the same way that the shrewd manager was justifying himself before the debtors while robbing his master, the Pharisees were justifying themselves in the eyes of others, but their Master knows their hearts. And as detestable as stealing was to the earthly master, the Pharisees' actions and attitudes were detestable to God. And in the same way that the master was relieving his manager of managing his business, God was also relieving the Jewish nation, represented here by the Pharisees, from managing his work in the world.

In closing, I believe that this parable was meant for the Pharisees, and that through it Jesus was teaching two messages. One message was about the need to repent from the love of money and thus gain entry to eternal dwellings, and the other was the fact that the Pharisees could not be entrusted with the message of grace or "true riches," because they had been dishonest with the Law or "worldly wealth." Sadly, the Pharisees, despite their best attempts at safeguarding the Law, were breaking it, and thus they were people of this world rather than people of light. Yet the Lord was not closing to them the door of salvation.

CHAPTER 19

The Message and the Approach
Jesus as The Word

GENESIS 2:4

When translating the Greek term *Logos* in John 1, most biblical translators render it as *The Word*. Sadly, this choice does not do justice to everything the rich term *Logos* offers.

We speak today of the Bible being the Word of God, meaning God-breathed and not human-breathed. We also think of the prophets of old as having transmitted to their people words from God. In both cases, all these words have become almost static and lifeless. They are words in black or red or other colors printed on paper, but they have become mere words.

My question is: How does Jesus as The Word compare or contrast with these words? Like his predecessors, the prophets of old, he also transmitted words from God. His words may have had more authority, power, and life, but here again, we have taken those words and put them in a book that we call the New Testament.

It is not my intention to do away with either the Old Testament or the New Testament. It is also not my intention to have us simply memorize Scripture so that we no longer need to read it as static printed words. Even then, we would have only transported static words from the printed page to our brains!

Before I explain myself, I will ask that we read John 1, verses 1 and 14a: "In the beginning was the Word, and the Word was with God, and the Word was God. …The Word became flesh and made his dwelling among us." In verse 14, John moves us from the static to the living. He clothes The Word, as it were, with flesh and blood. The Word was never static. His words may have become static, but he has not. "A picture is worth a thousand words" is an English proverb. This is what John does in verse 14. He paints a picture for us, but it is not a static picture. This picture throbs with life. With it, John bridges an eternity. The eternal Word that was from the beginning, that was with God and that was God, has come to dwell among us.

How else could humans ever know God as he is? Had John stopped short of verse 14, we would have continued to discuss to this day what Logos means, how best to translate it, and what it may mean for us. But now, as The Word is robed in flesh and blood, we can know and touch God. This is how the same John expressed this thought in 1 John 1:1: "That which was from the beginning, which we have heard, which we have seen with our eyes, which we have looked at and our hands have touched—this we proclaim concerning the Word of life." The "Word of life" here is the incarnated Word of life. As in John 1:14, John is speaking of Jesus incarnate, not of the words of life that he spoke.

Now to the title of this section. Did Jesus carry a message when he walked on our earth? Was he entrusted with a message from heaven to deliver to earth? The answer to these questions is definitely yes. Jesus did carry a message. But that message was he, himself. He was the message, and his approach was the

Incarnation. In him, the message was not words alone. It was his very person. His life was a living demonstration, the actualization of the love, compassion, and grace of God.

I do not mean hereby to belittle the words of wisdom or truth that he pronounced. But if we were to reduce him to his words, we would be doing him and ourselves a gross injustice. For he did not only pronounce or proclaim truth, he was Truth. He was Life. He gave life because he was the Life. He spoke truth because he was the Truth. He did not show us the way. He was the Way. How else could he speak life into dead Lazarus? Or by the touch of his hand grant life to the widow's son according to Luke 7? Or how could a woman gain healing by simply touching his robe, unless he was Life himself?

What does that mean for us? How should that influence us as Christians? Sadly, we have reduced our lives to words. We speak and write words, and we put words into books, even as I am doing right now. In the end, not only do the words remain static, but our very lives can also become static. What we have done is exactly the reverse of the process that Jesus introduced when The Word became flesh. We have reversed that and turned our lives, our flesh, into words. We even hide behind words because our flesh might betray who we really are. Our lives, if we were to have them exposed, would betray us. It becomes a lot easier to mask them with words.

We may not realize or admit it, but the truth is that in the same way that Jesus was the message and the Incarnation was his approach, we also are our own message. We must individually decide what message we want to be as we flesh out his Word by the example of our lives.

CHAPTER 20

Water into Wine
Launching a Ministry from a Wedding

JOHN 2:1–11

Imagine for a moment the following headline in the *Capernaum Daily:* "Self-Professed Messiah Launches Ministry by Turning Water into Wine!" I think that every single copy of that paper would be sold because nobody in their right mind would do anything of this sort. Nobody in the history of the prophets of the Jewish nation had ever done anything even close. The least that can be said of what we read in John 2:1–11 is that this is a very strange way to launch one's ministry. By performing this miracle, Jesus was sending a very confusing message. Only six months before, a man appeared who was also claiming to have been sent by God. This man's name was John the Baptist. Unlike Jesus, John did not drink any wine. As a matter of fact, he did not even eat the foods his people ate. He had honey and wild locusts for breakfast, lunch, and dinner. Now someone else appears, also claiming to be a prophet, who not only drinks wine, but also makes it. The *Capernaum Daily* could have run another headline: "Weird Prophets: Locust-eater and Wine-maker."

What on earth was Jesus thinking?

This is a valid question. Did his mother twist his arm? Was it a desire for good wine during a party? Did he want to show off before those who had chosen to give him a chance and followed him to hear the things he said?

Human reasoning says that he was assassinating his own ministry before even properly launching it. He did not need bad publicity. He created his own. Who on earth would begin any type of trade by turning anything into wine? Is it that there were not enough drinking people in Israel, or that there was such a shortage of wine-makers? Or maybe Jesus was publicizing a new brand of wine that he could then turn into a profitable business? If so, what better place to do that than at a wedding, right?

All the questions above are valid, unless of course, we wholly misunderstand what was going on and totally miss the point of this miracle. Let's give this a try and ask a few important questions.

Our first question is: Why doesn't Jesus perform his first miracle in a synagogue or at the Temple? Or maybe even out in the open? Why at a wedding?

The second question concerns what "hour" Jesus was referring to when he told his mother "my hour has not come" (John 2:4). He could not be referring to the hour of performing a miracle since he did perform one. As the reader of the New Testament will note in other texts, this would not be the last time Jesus speaks of "the hour" or "his hour." Those comments usually referred to his death. But what association was there between what Mary was asking him to do and the hour of his death? Why would he bring this into the discussion in the first place?

Unmoved by his seemingly cold answer, Mary then turned to the servants and said to do whatever Jesus tells them. Looking at the stone jars nearby, Jesus ordered the servants to fill them with water. I find it intriguing and quite astonishing that Jesus would spell out the type of liquid that should go into those jars. It would have been obvious to everyone, and especially to the servants who had been used to filling those jars with water every time their masters went to the Temple to pray. They surely did not need Jesus to specify that the jars be filled with water. That is what those jars were for. They had never been used for anything but water. Which brings us to a third question: Why was Jesus that explicit about using water?

No sooner had the servants filled these jars than Jesus told them to draw some out and begin to serve. Now we need to ask: At what point did the water turn into wine? All we have is the testimony of the master of the banquet. He didn't know what had happened, but he gave a wonderful testimony of the excellent quality of this new wine.

We have here four important elements from which we can begin to build the true meaning behind this miracle: wedding, hour, water, and wine. If there is one key element in these four, it would be the word "hour." This word will open the door to a correct interpretation of this passage.

As noted above, the "hour" as used by Jesus always referred to the time appointed by God for completing the work of redemption. With that in mind, Jesus was forthright in his answer that his "hour" had not yet come. The work of redemption was still three-plus years away. His time to hang on a cross and shed his blood was not here yet.

But let us remember that it was for this "hour" that he had come. This explains why the "hour" was on his mind from day one. It follows that everything that Jesus did was connected to this hour for which he had come. And here at the wedding was his first chance to begin to paint a picture of what that would mean.

The water that always filled those stone jars was used for ceremonial purification. The Book of Leviticus gives the details of the washings required before a worshipper could access the Temple grounds. What Jesus does is turn that water for purification into wine, which in the New Testament context refers to his blood. So, while the cross was still three-plus years away, Jesus would use the occasion to begin to pave the way for a new covenant made with this new "wine." Water for purification will no longer be needed. Jesus will replace it with his blood.

But why did Jesus do that at a wedding party? Why not wait until the Last Supper and then explain it all to his disciples? I suspect that Jesus was using the occasion for a picture of a more glorious wedding, the wedding recorded for us in the Book of Revelation 19:9, namely the "wedding supper of the Lamb." Jesus launched his ministry with a mini celebration of that coming day. Isn't this what he referred to at the Last Supper when he passed the cup of wine to his disciples saying, "I tell you, I will not drink from this fruit of the vine from now on until that day when I drink it new with you in my Father's kingdom" (Matthew 26:29)? To choose a wedding party and to change water into wine was not the most absurd thing a prophet of God could do, regardless of what the *Capernaum Daily* might think. In fact, it was the most amazing prophetic miracle of what was and is to come.

CHAPTER 21

Meaning vs. Definition
How to Change Lives

JOHN 8:2-11

In real life, we are rarely challenged to define words or attitudes. Maybe when we were made to sit in our English class or some other language class, but not in regular life. Instead, what we are daily challenged to do is to give meaning to our words or our attitudes. But how different is a definition from meaning? Enormous! And nothing could better represent that than the life of Jesus. Here are a couple of examples.

According to John 8:2-11, Jesus was put on the spot in how to deal with a woman who was caught in adultery. The teachers of the Law and the Pharisees were trying to trap him because the Law of Moses, according to them, meant only one thing: stoning this woman to death. How should Jesus respond? How about giving a definition of the word "forgiveness" or the definition of "giving someone a second chance"? Or maybe Jesus could have given a lecture on forgiveness or, even better, quoted Scripture to counter the claims of the accusers? He would be answering the Law by citing the Law.

Yet Jesus did not do any of the above. What he did was give meaning to the word "forgiveness" by forgiving this woman. He told her, "Neither do I condemn you." If anybody, Jesus had the full authority to judge her. But he did not. He actualized what it means to give someone a second chance by giving this woman a second chance; that is, by saying to her, "Go now and leave your life of sin" (John 8:11b). He did not see the need to explain himself or to justify his actions. He just did it! This is when meaning takes on real life. This is when meaning becomes meaningful.

We find another example in Luke 7:11–15, in which Jesus raised an only son from the dead. Jesus said only two words to the mother: "Don't cry." Then he went and touched the bier, raised the boy, and gave him back to his mother. Did Jesus expound on the definition of the word *compassion*? No, he didn't. He gave it meaning. After all, the widow did not want or need a definition. She did not need words, even words of comfort. She needed something much more meaningful: a human touch. That was exactly what Jesus offered as he touched the son's bier.

How about Jesus' tears at the death of his friend Lazarus, or his touch of a leper, or the mud he put on the blind man's eyes? The meanings Jesus gave with his actions are too many to list in this short study. These were true meanings of love, compassion, forgiveness, and so much else.

The world in which we live could not care less about what we know. It could not care less if we passed all our exams successfully. The world's questions and expectations are not answered in black ink on white sheets of paper. Our sick world is hurting and dying, and its questions are written in sweat and in blood. Our world does not need more definitions of love or compassion or forgiveness. It doesn't want to know how we understand the Trinity, or how we interpret John 3:16, or what it means to be born again. Rather, it wants to see the true meaning of these

Christian values. It wants to be able to recognize the ways in which our claim of being born again has transformed our lives. It wants to see a living proof thereof.

Let me put it differently. How about explaining in words and defining what warmth means to someone who is sitting in the cold? Or how about explaining in words the red rose bush or green shrubbery that is outside the window of a patient sitting in a hospital bed? One could use the best dictionaries on the market and even translate the definition into several languages, but how meaningful would this be to the person? Would it not be more meaningful to open the curtains by his bed? Would it not be more meaningful to take him outside and allow him to feel the warmth of the sun on his body? That is the difference between definition and meaning.

Jesus, the best teacher who ever lived on planet earth, did not waste his time giving definitions to the values that he lived or to the truths that he believed and came to teach. He gave meaning. To those who were touched by his life, that meaning became meaningful, worthwhile, and life-changing. May we follow his example!

CHAPTER 22

Recognizing Jesus
Agape and *Philo*

JOHN 21

When Jesus appeared to his disciples at the Sea of Galilee, they didn't recognize him. (See John 21:1–9.) In verse 8, John states that their boat was not far from the shore; yet, for some reason, the disciples did not recognize Jesus.

I suppose, if I am to give Peter and his cohorts the benefit of the doubt, that when Jesus did show up on the shore that morning, it may have been still hazy. The sun may not have fully risen yet. So, their chances of recognizing him may have been somewhat dimmed by the weather or by the time of day. To allow even more benefit, I suppose that with those seven men working all night, the last thing they expected was someone calling to them from the shore. Their minds were still busy trying to figure out where all the fish they had expected to catch the night before had gone. Or perhaps, they were just too tired, so that when Jesus appeared on the scene, they did not pay much attention to speech or speaker. We will give them all that.

On the other hand, Jesus had spent three-plus years in ministry. Except for those times when he was conversing with his Father, and the times when others were around him also, Jesus had spent between 80 and 85 percent of his time with the Twelve. How many times had they heard him preach and teach? One would imagine that his voice was as familiar to them as their own voices. It becomes extremely striking that on the shore that morning, as he called out to them, they just could not recognize his voice any longer.

Had his voice changed between the last time they had seen him and now? He was only gone for a few days. They could not possibly have forgotten how his voice sounded. I seriously doubt that he had become taller or shorter after his Resurrection. I also doubt very much that his skin color had changed, or that the color of his hair was different, or that he had gotten a haircut!

Jesus then tells them to throw their nets on the right side of their boat, and they will find some fish. I want to stop here for a minute. There were three professional fishermen in the group, namely Peter, James, and John. Why on earth would they listen to and heed the words of a stranger? What could he know that they didn't? Why waste their time? They should have stopped at that instant and tried to find out who it was that seemed so confident. But they didn't bother. I honestly do not have an explanation for such behavior. If they were such bad fishermen from the start, why not find another profession? Without giving their minds the time to think, they do what this stranger tells them.

The miracle happens, but that does not mean that everyone has the heart to understand. They catch so many fish that they were unable to haul the net to the shore. The Sea of Galilee was Peter's second home. Being a fisherman by profession, he had spent more time on this body of water than anywhere else. It was here that Jesus had called him to follow him. It was here that Jesus had gone into Peter's boat and asked him to go into deep water and cast his nets. The catch was so big that day that his nets and the nets of his partners James and John began to break, and their boats began to sink. Had Peter forgotten all that? Was he so old that he had begun losing his memory? Or was something else more serious going on?

I make these observations in light of the fact that even with this new miracle, Peter was still unaware of the identity of the man on the shore. His eyes were open, but he could not see. His ears were clean of wax, but he could not hear. Most importantly, his heart just could not understand. It took John, the son of Zebedee, to alert him by saying, "It is the Lord" (John 21:7).

I guess I am shaming Peter, although this is definitely not my intention. I only want to ask why. What is it that allowed John, who is not blameless either, to finally recognize Jesus? What was John's secret? Both Peter and John had spent the same amount of time with their Master. There must be something John had that Peter was missing all along.

The answer to that critical question is found in John 21:20: "Peter turned and saw that the disciple whom Jesus loved was following them." (This was the one who had leaned back against Jesus at the supper and had said, "Lord, who is going to betray you?")

Peter had learned to follow Jesus. That was good enough for him. John went one step beyond. He learned to lean on him, to be close to his heart. That is the difference between a disciple who is in close fellowship with Jesus and one who is not.

That also explains why we, at times, have a hard time hearing and seeing Jesus, even though he is always speaking and always active in our lives. Our hearts have been dimmed. We are too busy catching fish in the seas of this world, so that even when a miracle happens, we are not able to recognize the one behind it. When will we learn, like John, to lean on Jesus and hear his heart? We may have learned to follow him, but we may have to begin to learn to also lean on him.

John 21 closes with a private talk between Jesus and Peter in which Jesus asks Peter the same question three times: "Do you love me?" Many commentators have argued that the reason for asking Peter the same question three times mirrors the fact that Peter had denied Jesus three times. In this view, the objective of that private encounter was to reinstate Peter.

Peter, having gone back to his old job as a fisherman, certainly needed a renewed calling to drop that job and be committed to fishing for people. In this private encounter, Jesus does exactly that, challenging him to feed his sheep. Yet, given Peter's failure to recognize who was behind the miraculous catch of fish, the Lord had to drive the point home. Peter's failure was due to the absence of intimacy. That explains the variance in the verb "to love" that the Lord uses in his three questions.

In his first and second questions, the Lord uses the Greek term *agape*, which denotes sacrificial love. Peter answers with a less intimate type of love, namely *philo*, or affection. Asking Peter a third time, the Lord then uses that second term, as well.

We also have some type of affection toward Jesus, but is that enough to recognize his voice? Is that enough to see him working in our lives? Could it be that, like Peter, our problem is the absence of an intimate relationship with him? Such an intimate relationship will help us not only to recognize him, as John did, but also protect us from denying him, as Peter did. An intimate relationship with Jesus is the antidote to many ills and problems, including sin.

It is interesting to note that Jesus never pushed Peter to confess or even to repent of having denied him three times. Rather, Jesus challenged Peter to a more intimate relationship with him. That is also our challenge today.

CHAPTER 23

Peter and Jonah
What Changes Us?

ACTS 10

I wonder under whose tutelage Jonah sat? Who were his role models and his teachers? Like others from his tribe and countrymen, he must have attended Sabbath prayers, and possibly read the Torah. He would not have been able to read the prophetic writings, because only Joel, one of the Minor Prophets, ministered before he did. The great prophet Isaiah came after he was gone.

Now, compare or contrast Jonah's circumstances with those of Peter who, for three years, sat under the tutelage of the Lord Jesus himself. Peter heard his master deliver the Great Commission of Matthew 28:18–20! Peter was exclusively promised the keys of the kingdom of heaven! (See Matthew 16:19.) Peter experienced the anointing of the Holy Spirit on the day of Pentecost! There is not much to compare between the two, is there?

However, let's look at Acts 10:1–30. On the surface, these verses contain the story of a centurion named Cornelius who took Peter into his home, but they also deal with the idea of ritual purity and impurity. To someone willing to spend time digging more deeply into the Word with the help of the Holy Spirit, some things begin to surface.

Let me try to unpack this. First, both men—Jonah and Peter—"happened to be" in the same city, namely Joppa, a seaside town. In Jewish thinking, the sea refers to the gentile world, whereas the land refers to the Jewish nation.

Second, both men were called to serve on a very special mission. Jonah was called to go to the Assyrian capital, Nineveh, at a time when the Assyrians were Israel's archenemy. In fact, the Ninevites were preparing to invade Israel and carry away its young citizenry into captivity. The Assyrian army conquered Samaria less than twenty years after Jonah visited Nineveh.

Peter, on the other hand, was called to visit the home of a Roman centurion, who was, by definition a Gentile, an enemy to Israel, and an occupier of the land. As a centurion, Cornelius had a hundred soldiers under him who enforced the continued occupation of Israel and the oppression of its citizens. Rome was no friend to the Jews. A few years later after Peter's encounter with Cornelius, Titus the Roman would encircle Jerusalem with his troops and destroy the Jewish Temple. killing and maiming many people and causing a new exile of the Jews.

But what is most interesting is the reaction of both men to their commissions. Jonah, steeped in his national Jewish attitude, could not get himself to go to the "other." The Ninevites were definitely "other." It took a storm, a whale, and a near-death experience to make him go.

Peter, also with his Jewish national and religious attitude, was not naturally disposed to go to the home of a Gentile. He makes his position clear as he enters the home of Cornelius: "You are well aware that it is against our law for a Jew to associate with or visit a Gentile" (Acts 10:28).

Even after spending three-plus years with Jesus, and even after the advent of the Holy Spirit on the day of Pentecost, Peter continued to consider himself a Jew. One obvious reason is that the term "Christian" was not yet in use. But the true reason is that Jewish nationalism was deeply embedded in Peter. Suffice it to remember how Paul confronted Peter in Antioch and publicly accused him of not acting in line with the truth of the Gospel. (See Galatians 2:11–14.)

For God to make Peter come to the house of Cornelius, he had to intervene in person: not through a storm or a whale like he did with Jonah, but with a vision. Three times in a row God would remind Peter of his love for all. His grace was able to make the impure pure and to turn an enemy into a brother.

So how did Jesus change Peter's natural nationalistic disposition? How did the advent of the Holy Spirit transform Peter's perspective toward others, especially the Gentiles?

The short answer is that neither the company and teachings of Jesus nor the outpouring of the Holy Spirit brought about such drastic changes in Peter. It took Peter many years of growing and maturing before he would write in his epistle: "But you are a chosen people, a royal priesthood, a holy nation, God's special possession, that you may declare the praises of him who called you out of darkness into his wonderful light. Once you were not a people, but now you are the people of God; once you had not received mercy, but now you have received mercy" (1 Peter 2:9–10).

It may be argued that Peter wrote his letter to believers from a Jewish background. However, when we look more closely at the two verses, we may wonder why Peter would say of such Jewish believers that "once you were not a people, but now you are the people of God." Rather, such a statement would much better apply to Christians from a non-Jewish background; that is, to Gentiles. This letter was written toward the end of Peter's life. It is so telling that it seemingly took him a lifetime to finally see the Gentiles as equal brothers and sisters in the faith, as the people of God.

Am I picking on Jonah? Or am I picking on Peter? I am not picking on either one. I am only using them as examples for us today.

The Assyrian Empire is no more. The Roman Empire is also no more. But, each of us may have our own "Assyrian" or "Roman" enemy. There is Palestinian and there is Jew. There is black and there is white. There is Japanese and there is Chinese. And the list goes on. Thankfully we will always have some friends. But sadly, we will also always have people whom we consider enemies, outcast, or simply "other."

While becoming a Christian can and does change us, that change is sometimes only temporary and incomplete. Not only does our spirit need to be born again, but also our minds, attitudes, prejudices, pocketbooks, and a host of other things.

So what is the answer? I think it is Christian maturity. It is developing the character of our Lord and Master, and that takes time. However, we would be wrong if we thought that time alone will guarantee our Christian maturity. Christian maturity does take time, but it also takes discipline, integrity, and, most importantly, a closeness of fellowship with Christ, the One whom we imitate.

CHAPTER 24

Understanding God's Action

Seeing the Bigger Picture

ACTS 12

When we have difficulty understanding certain actions of God, we tend to simply push them under the rug. We may also attempt to find reasons or even excuses for God's behavior. I am sure we have good intentions. We do not want to accuse God of anything ungodly.

The examples in Scripture of such instances are rare, but they are there. One such example occurs in Acts 12:1–24. The account tells us that Herod had James (the brother of John) killed, and then arrested Peter. An angel rescued Peter, and Herod was unable to locate him.

The question that has puzzled me for quite some time is this: Why did God allow James to be put to death, while he intervened to save Peter? We cannot accuse God of favoritism. He is above that. But then how do we explain it to the family of James? If I were in their shoes, I would wonder why God did not intervene on his behalf in the same way that he did on Peter's behalf.

In our attempts to justify the killing of the one and the miraculous escape of the other, some of us will probably turn to verse 5, where Luke interrupts the story with this statement: "So Peter was kept in prison, but the church was earnestly praying to God for him."

In light of this verse, we might infer that it was the church's earnest prayer that got Peter out of prison, but that carries the subtle, unspoken assumption that nobody really cared about James. So, when Herod threw him in jail, the church did not bother to pray. According to this explanation, the big secret is prayer, specifically the church's prayer. There was no favoritism on the part of God, only carelessness on the part of the church. God is vindicated and the church is vilified.

I suppose this would be one way to explain what happened. But does this explanation stand on solid ground? To answer that, we need to look at the text more closely. For God to answer prayer, the most basic component, according to Holy Writ, is to have faith. James, among others, brings this out very clearly in his epistle. We wonder how much faith there was within the praying church in Jerusalem when the servant Rhoda told them that Peter was at the door. Their response exposes not their faith, but, rather, their faithlessness: You're out of your mind" (Acts 12:15). To them, it was his spirit—the spirit of someone who was already dead. The general belief was that for the three days following someone's death, that person's spirit kept roaming around. To the church, Peter was dead. Full stop!

In the meantime, that spirit kept knocking on their door. It is one thing for a spirit to roam for three days, but knocking on people's doors was not something spirits did or were supposed to do. Whether out of fear or out of curiosity, others besides Rhoda went to the door. Upon seeing Peter, they were astonished.

I would guess the expressions of astonishment on their faces hid expressions of shame inside their hearts. Had their faith been activated in prayer, they would have jumped for joy. God was answering their prayers. They knew that God was going to do something. As a matter of fact, they were praying and waiting for that knock on the door. They would have expected Peter, and not his spirit, to show up!

But alas, that was not the case. The members of the church were praying, but they lacked the faith to see their prayers answered. It was clearly not their prayers that moved the hand of God and sent the angel Peter's way that morning.

That brings us back to square one. How can we accept, explain, or justify the fact that God did not intervene on behalf of James while he did on behalf of Peter? While we do not know for sure whether or not the church prayed for the release of James, we know that it definitely wasn't the church's prayer for Peter that got him out of his prison cell. To absolve God of any show of favoritism, we should look for another more plausible explanation.

In our study of the Bible, we often are not careful enough to look at the context, whether immediate, intermediate or distant. These are always an essential and critical key to a proper understanding of the text in question. So, let's look at the immediate context of this story.

Luke introduces us to the evil intents of King Herod in verse 1: "It was about this time that King Herod arrested some who belonged to the church." It is true that Herod went against James and then against Peter. But in fact, he was going not against individuals but against the church. He meant to destroy the church and cause it to crumble. If he could get rid of the church leadership, the church would cease to flourish and maybe even cease to exist. Crush the foundations and the whole building would come down.

This is not a wild idea I am conjuring up to argue against the accusation of God's favoritism. This is the whole message of the Book of Acts: God building his church. To help prove my point, turn to verse 24, the closing verse of this incident. Luke, guided by the Holy Spirit, writes: "But the word of God continued to spread and flourish." This chapter is introduced with an attack on the church. It closes with God causing his Word and his church to flourish.

Let me sum this up. We would be dead wrong if we think that the Bible, or more specifically the Book of Acts, is about people. It is not. This is a book about God, moving in the world, fulfilling his plan and using people to accomplish his plan. This episode is not about James or Peter. Bible publishers who call this event "Peter's miraculous escape from prison" get it wrong. It is true that James and Peter are two characters in the story. But the main unseen character is God, and if there is a second important character, it would be his church. By that I do not mean the local Jerusalem church at the time, but rather the global church that has always been on the heart of God, even before the creation of the world! Neither Herod, nor anyone like him, will ever be able to stop its expansion and growth, let alone eliminate it. This was the promise that Jesus made when he said that the "gates of Hades will not overcome [the church]" (Matthew 16:18). Gates do not attack because they are not an offensive weapon. They are meant as defensive mechanisms in the face of attacks. Yet faced with the advance of the church, those defenses will just not do. The gates of hell will not withstand the advance of the church.

What does this mean for us today? We may think that humanity is the central player on the world stage. We may think that we are the center of the universe. I am sorry to say this cannot be further from the truth. This is not to belittle the role that God has for us. It is not to make us little robots used to fulfill God's plan. After all, we are created in his image and we have important roles. But we must be willing to accept whatever he has planned for us, not grudgingly, but with joy, for we are part of a much larger mosaic, a much larger picture. Our piece in it, whether small or large, is only one piece. For us to allow him in his infinite wisdom to fit our piece into his larger frame is to see his glory manifested, and our ultimate eternal good.

If that sounds too harsh, remember John the Baptist and his lot. I am not talking about the fact that his head was also chopped off, like James. Rather, I am talking about the fact that his ministry was terminated before it could germinate in human terms. The only explanation is that John had completed the role God had planned for him. His time to go had arrived.

While we're at it, why not push the envelope some more and think of the Lord himself? Was his lot any better than that of John the Baptist or James? Not only was his cup much more bitter than theirs as he hung on the Cross, but he also had his life cut short after only three short years of ministry. How much more good he could have done if he had lived a little longer! But alas, the Father's plan for his own Son was also completed.

Thus, we dare not question the wisdom of God as he allowed Herod to behead James and miraculously get Peter out. This is not and has never been about favoritism. If it were, the One who would have been most favored would have been his only Son. Yet even he was not spared.

If we are still here, it is definitely for a reason. That reason is not to fill one more seat in a church pew. It is not to make another dollar in the stock market. Rather it is to fulfill God's plan in and for our lives, with the ultimate goal being his glory and the advancement of his church on earth.

CHAPTER 25

Symptoms and Sin
God's True Justice

GALATIANS 5:19–21

My dad lived to be 119 years of age. He was born in 1892 and passed away on January 27, 2011. Let's suppose that from the day he was born until the day he died, he was sinning before God. That would make a lifetime of sinning: all 119 years of sinning. Let's also suppose that my dad did not repent, and so according to Scripture, he will be condemned to an eternity in hell. Except that creates a huge dilemma for God. For how can a just God punish a lifetime of sinning with an eternity of damnation? That would not be fair, would it?

God himself set the rules of revenge or punishment in his Word. According to Exodus 21, Leviticus 24, and Deuteronomy 19, the principle was laid out very clearly. "Eye for eye, tooth for tooth, hand for hand, foot for foot," and so on. A just judge cannot pass the same sentence against someone who has committed a homicide and someone else who has exceeded the speed limit. Though both may end up in jail, their sentences would be vastly different. Our legal system leads the judge to hand down a sentence commensurate with the crime committed. God cannot take revenge on someone's temporal sin, whatever sin that may be, with an eternity in hell. It is not commensurate. In other words, if God is not punishing temporal sin with a punishment lasting an eternity, then what exactly is God punishing?

Biblical expositors and students have come up with several answers to the puzzling question of eternal punishment. One of those is that since sin is committed against a great person, namely God himself, the punishment would also be great. According to this, the greater the party against whom sin is committed, the greater the punishment. Another possible answer is that in the same way that God rewards repentant people with an eternity in heaven, so he punishes unrepentant people with an eternity in hell.

While there may be some truth to both of these answers, there must be a more convincing answer. God must have solid unquestionable reasons that would allow him to accept someone into his heaven, and order someone else to hell.

The answer has nothing to do with the duration of someone's sin. I gave the example of my father's long life. It would be the same judgment against someone living only a few years and dying without having repented of his or her sins. The Bible does not differentiate between those two elements, nor between what we may consider bigger sins versus smaller sins. That, by itself, poses a big question regarding the severity of God's punishment.

The answer to this dilemma lies elsewhere. It begins with a proper understanding of what constitutes sin. What we call sin, regardless of the nature of the act, is, in fact, only a symptom of the true nature of sin. In that sense, killing, lying, stealing, lusting, and every other name we give to such acts are all symptoms. They are not in and of themselves the problem. They are only the outward expression of the true problem.

In Galatians 5:19–21, Paul lists what he calls the "acts of the flesh." While the same acts may be called sins in other places in the Bible, Paul describes them in a totally different way. To him, those sins, whether discord, jealousy, hatred, or others, are only outward acts of the flesh. In Scripture, the term "flesh" refers to humanity without God: humankind following after its carnal desires.

In verses 22 and 23, Paul outlines what he calls the "fruit of the Spirit," including love, joy, peace and the other virtues. Here again, they are outward expressions of something invisible; namely, the Spirit. The term "Spirit," with an uppercase S, does not refer to the human spirit. Rather, it refers to the Holy Spirit of God, who, when ruling human life, bears the fruits Paul mentions. Fruit is not something you stick to a fruit tree. Rather, it is something that a tree produces on its own when it is well watered.

So, is God punishing the acts of the flesh, the outward expressions of the real problem? That would not make sense, would it? Moreover, if God was punishing the symptoms with an eternity in hell, he would have to create different types of hell for different offenders. Each offender would then be sent to a specific hell according to his or her offense. A serial killer's hell would not be comparable to that of someone who has stolen a few dollars, or even robbed a bank. In the same way that judges sentence a felony differently than a misdemeanor, we expect God to judge differently according to the sin.

So, what is God punishing, regardless of the act itself, with an eternity in hell? Similarly, what is God rewarding with an eternity in heaven? The answer lies in the nature of sin. Sin is, at its core, our emphatic independence of God: our desire to be separated from God. Sin denies God his lordship over one's life. If someone has chosen in his or her lifetime to be separated and independent from God, the only logical and biblical result following that principle is to continue to be separated from God. Understood in that way, it is not God who is sentencing us to an eternity away from himself.

Rather, we are going there on our own feet and legs. God, despite being the almighty, respects our decision and will not force himself on anyone.

Based on the understanding above, it logically follows that if someone has chosen to invite God into his or her life, opting to have a relationship with God, such a person would spend an eternity in heaven with him. Again, this is not based on any good act because nothing is good enough to earn such an honor. Separation begets separation, and fellowship begets fellowship.

Two important issues flow out of this discussion. First, what happens to someone who has opted to be in fellowship with God, but then has fallen into sin? Secondly, what is the key to overcoming sinful behavior?

The answer to the first question is this: If, by sin, we mean the symptoms of our sinful nature regardless of what that sin may be, then these need to be treated as symptoms. I have already pointed out that sin is our decision to be independent of God. While it is true that what we usually call sin is only a byproduct of a deeper problem, we should bear in mind that a temporary rift or fracture in our relationship with God can be the cause of such sinful behavior. That explains the apparent dichotomy we find in the First Letter of John. In 1 John 1:8–10, John speaks of those who have established a relationship with God and who have made the decision to allow God to rule their lives. However, there will be times when those people will temporarily lose fellowship with God and fall into sinful behavior: "If we claim to be without sin, we deceive ourselves and the truth is not in us. If we confess our sins, he is faithful and just and will forgive us our sins and purify us from all unrighteousness. If we claim we have not sinned, we make him out to be a liar and his word is not in us."

In 1 John 3:6, he speaks of a totally different group: those who have made the decision to be independent of God. This is not a temporary rift. It is rather a conscious decision not to have a relationship from the start: "No one who lives in him keeps on sinning. No one who continues to sin has either seen him or known him."

So, what is the key to overcoming sinful behavior? The answer to this important question is so simple and so obvious, but before I get to it, there is an important point to elucidate. This is the notion that preachers often mention: the rift in fellowship with God as a consequence of sinful behavior. While that is true, what is even truer and more basic is the reverse: A rift in fellowship with God results in sinful behavior.

The key to overcoming sinful behavior is to be in constant fellowship with God. That is the only antidote: nothing less, nothing else, and nothing more.

During those times in which we fall into sinful behavior, when we allow symptoms of our independence from God and our lack of fellowship with him to rule the day, we don't need to repent of those symptoms. Rather, we need to repent of our independence and fall back into his arms.

When we call for repentance, we are usually referring to repenting of symptoms. By virtue of doing that, we have unintentionally "upgraded" sin. Independence from God is much more serious than any bad behavior, no matter how serious that behavior may be in our eyes. It is because of this one true sin that many will spend eternity separated from God.

CHAPTER 26

God Bless You!
Mixing Up Our Tenses

EPHESIANS 1:3

Back when I was attending elementary school, my English language teachers taught us the difference in tenses. Initially, it was all past, present, and future. When we moved up classes, we discovered tenses were a little more complex than we had originally thought. Now we had to learn present continuous, past perfect, and a lot more.

Speakers and writers are careful not to mix tenses lest they end up giving mixed messages. Tenses are an integral part of proper expression, comprehension, and application. I am not an English teacher, and this is not meant to be an introduction to English grammar. I bring this up to help us discover together how a careless observation of a certain conjugated verb can have drastic implications in our lives.

First, let me begin by sharing a personal testimony that dates back almost fifty years. At the time, my parents and I were living in Jerusalem. I was about nineteen or twenty years of age and had only accepted Christ as my personal Savior a year or two before that date.

A Christian gentleman who lived close to us often came ringing our doorbell. For various reasons, I did not care to see this brother when he came to visit, but, there were not too many Evangelical Christians in Jerusalem whom he could visit.

I had a bad attitude, and I knew it. I even confessed it on a regular basis. Every night as I knelt beside my bed, I would ask God to grant me love for this brother. In my heart of hearts, I wanted to love this brother. I had nothing against him. But I could not get my feelings for him to warm up. My prayers were not readily answered. I continued to struggle with this attitude for weeks.

In my sincere attempts to resolve this problem, one day I picked up a small book from our church library. I do not recall the title or author. Halfway through, I decided that it was not for me. Though the book was not mine to dispose of, I dumped it anyway. I didn't want anyone to become as hypocritical as that book seemed to be leading me to act.

The author gave his opinion that it was simple to love someone you do not love or care for. Just act as if you do. In other words, put on the face and smile of someone who cares and loves when meeting someone you do not love or care about, and the miracle will happen. Immediately after reading this chapter, I decided to throw the book away. Why would I add hypocrisy to my other sins and shortcomings?

Thankfully, my stepmom did not pick up the trash the next day. So, I decided, for lack of other options, to pick up the book again and continue reading. It was then that I learned something new, something that had never crossed my mind as a young Christian.

It was as if the author, in the chapter that followed, knew exactly the type of protest or question the reader might have to what he had written earlier. He began by explaining what hypocrisy is and is not. That had been my exact issue with his book when I threw it away. To be hypocritical, he wrote, meant that the way you act is against your will. In other words, if you do not have the will to love someone, and you wear a smile on your face when you see them, that would be hypocritical. But if you do have the will to love someone, but your feelings are out of whack when you wear a smile on your face, you are not being hypocritical because you are aligning your action (in this case, your smile) with your will.

As I looked into my heart that day, realizing that I had asked the Lord every night before going to bed to grant me love for that brother, I knew I had the will. I wanted to love him. I asked to love him. My problem was that my feelings were out of line. I didn't know how to align my feelings with my will.

In closing, the author suggested a very simple formula. Continue putting a smile on your face, even though you do not feel like it, and within a week or two, see if your feelings line up with your will. To my amazement, two weeks after reading that book, I discovered that his formula worked, even beyond my expectations. My attitude toward this brother's visits to our home changed drastically. If, for whatever reason, he did not come one week, I would be the one knocking on his door. We became strong friends until the day he passed away.

Now, let's return to our English grammar, and the practical implications of a proper understanding of one simple verb, and how that can affect our lives now and forever more.

In Ephesians 1:3, Paul writes, "Praise be to the God and Father of our Lord Jesus Christ, who has blessed us in the heavenly realms with every spiritual blessing in Christ."

We note in the above verse that the conjugated verb "bless" is in the present perfect tense. This tense expresses an action that was started in the past and continues in the present. For example, I might say that my wife Evelyn and I have been married for forty-five years. The action was completed forty-five years ago when the Lebanese pastor blessed our union, but we are still married to this day. In the context of Ephesians 1, Paul says that God has already blessed us—past completed action that continues to the present—with every spiritual blessing in Christ. The action has been completed and it is still true!

Let's look at the word "bless." I have a very hard time when I speak at a church and I am made to stand at the door to shake people's hands as they exit. My difficulty is not shaking people's hands; rather, it is with the greeting they offer as they do it—God bless you! I also have a hard time when sitting at the dinner table and hearing someone pray that God will bless the food. While I always appreciate giving thanks for the provision of food and friends, I do not quite understand what is meant when someone prays to the Lord to bless the food. What do we want God to do? Multiply it to make it feed many more? Use it to nourish our bodies? Keep us from germs and other bad bacteria? I am not sure. I feel the same way when I hear the words, "God bless America." What do we want God to do with our nation?

In short, it seems to me that we both misuse and abuse the word "bless." The word has lost its meaning because we use it all the time without really knowing what we mean. We also do not know what others mean when they use this word.

So, let us go back to Ephesians. Following verse 3, Paul explains in more detail how God "has blessed us." Among these blessings is the fact that God "chose us . . . to be holy and blameless" (1:4). God also predestined us for adoption" (1:5). In 1:7–8, Paul says, "In him we have redemption through his blood, the forgiveness of sins, in accordance with the riches of God's grace that he lavished on us." Here we are, continually asking for forgiveness, love, joy, peace, and so on, when in fact, these have already been lavished on us. Once we have accepted Christ in our lives and have become the children of God, all the riches of his grace have already been placed in our account.

What does all the above mean? What are the implications for us?

First of all, in terms of sins, we do not earn our forgiveness. Our forgiveness has been granted based on the redemption of Christ. We confess our sins before God, we repent of these sins, and then, in faith, we enjoy his forgiveness regardless of whether or not we feel we are forgiven. We have his promise in 1 John 1:9 that "if we confess our sins, he is faithful and just and will forgive us our sins and purify us from all unrighteousness."

Believing this promise means acting on it. It means living out the forgiveness that we have already received: the forgiveness that he has already lavished on us and that has already been placed in our account. These actions have all been completed. That is why it was important to note the present perfect tense of the verbs above. We cannot and should not live with guilt and shame, as long as we do not have unconfessed sins in our lives.

In doing counseling over the years, I have discovered that Christians who suffer from such problems as depression will almost always get better if and when they grasp and begin to actualize in their lives what it means to live the promises of God in faith regardless of their feelings or circumstances.

How about love, joy, or peace? How about the practice of continuing to ask God to bless us with those things? It is not only hard to understand what is meant, but it is also shocking. What else do we want God to bless us with, that he has not already blessed us with? We know that God's promises are true. We accept the Bible as his Word to us. Therefore, it must be our lack of understanding which has so negatively impacted and influenced our use of such verbs.

Lacking the proper understanding, we have continued to live always asking and imploring like beggars in the alleys of the Old City of Jerusalem. God is waiting for the time when we will understand. The secret to victorious Christian living is to live the promises of God in faith regardless of how we feel. Once our will is aligned with the will of God, as it is prescribed clearly in his Word, we can claim in full every blessing which God has both promised and granted.

Changing the Culture
What's a Christian to Do?

PHILEMON

It is estimated that between 30 and 40 percent of the inhabitants of Italy during the first century BC were slaves. Those numbers did not change much in the first century AD. One would, therefore, wonder what effect, if any, the Christian faith had on the Roman slave culture! Were the Apostles and the early Church Fathers indirectly guilty of propagating that culture rather than preaching a message of emancipation? Did not Peter and Paul condone the inhumanity of slavery when they addressed masters and slaves in their letters?

Here are a few passages in which Peter and Paul bring up the matter of slave and master.

> Slaves, obey your earthly masters with respect and fear, and with sincerity of heart, just as you would obey Christ. Obey them not only to win their favor when their eye is on you, but as slaves of Christ, doing the will of God from your heart. And masters, treat your slaves in the same way. Do not threaten them, since you know that he who is both

their Master and yours is in heaven, and there is no favoritism with him (Ephesians 6:5–6, 9).

Those who have believing masters should not show them disrespect just because they are fellow believers. Instead, they should serve them even better because their masters are dear to them as fellow believers and are devoted to the welfare of their slaves (1 Timothy 6:2).

Slaves, in reverent fear of God submit yourselves to your masters, not only to those who are good and considerate, but also to those who are harsh (1 Peter 2:18).

In Christ there is "neither slave nor free" (Galatians 3:28).

What are we to make of all the above? Here are a few observations.

The calling of both Peter and Paul was to present Christ and preach the Gospel. Getting involved in a social evil such as slavery, though badly needed, would have taken away from their message. Both men had to be true to their calling.

Given the huge number of slaves in Italy and in the Roman Empire in general, it was neither Peter's nor Paul's intention to start an insurrection against the rulers or against society. Just imagine what serious and unpredictable repercussions there would be if the message of the Gospel had an element of rousing the slaves against their masters in order to demand their emancipation!

Both Peter and Paul were addressing issues inside the church family. Even when they addressed sinful behavior or practices that were prevalent in society in general, it was in order to alert the church to steer away from such practices and behavior. In other words, it was not their intention to correct or straighten up the general culture, knowing full well that the world's culture is under the rule of Satan. Their message was to help Christians be salt and light who can change the culture from within. Peter's and Paul's message was not to call for social reformation, but for spiritual transformation. Such transformation will have the dynamism to change and reform culture.

The overarching principle in what Paul wrote to the believers was that in Christ social differences should cease to manifest themselves in the same way that they manifest themselves in the world. That did not mean that suddenly a slave ceased to be a slave, but that in a Christian context the slave should be treated as a brother in Christ. It meant that the attitude of a Christian master toward his slave should not be one of enslavement. The relationship between master and slave was now governed by the fact that before Christ both were slaves, having one Master, and as such, they were brothers.

With all this in mind, let's look at Paul's letter to Philemon. In it we have that concrete example of the Christian principles that should influence, regulate, and determine the relationship between master and slave. It's short, so I encourage you to read it on your own. The text is clear that Philemon owned a slave by the name of Onesimus. Apphia is assumed to be Philemon's wife and Archippus their son. We can surmise from verse 18 that Onesimus had robbed his master and ran away. Weeks or months later, and following another possible crime, this time in Rome, Onesimus lands in jail. Through a set of undisclosed circumstances, Onesimus meets Paul, who was under house arrest in the same city. During his time, Onesimus is introduced to the Christian faith and Paul becomes his spiritual father. Referring to Onesimus, Paul uses the endearing term "my son." The spirit of the letter is captured in verses 15 and 16: "Perhaps the reason he was separated from you for a little while was that you might have him back forever—no longer as a slave, but better than a slave, as a dear brother. He is very dear to me but even dearer to you, both as a fellow man and as a brother in the Lord."

There is equality within the church family. Onesimus was treated a slave before he came to know Christ, but now Paul expects Philemon, possibly the pastor of the flock that meets in his home, to treat the repentant Onesimus like he would treat any other member of his church; namely, as a brother in the Lord.

Paul goes even further in his appeal to Philemon, writing in verse 17: "So if you consider me a partner, welcome him as you would welcome me." This is quite shocking. If and when Paul visited Philemon's house, he would have been treated as an apostle and as a spiritual father to Philemon himself.

Paul is basically asking Philemon to treat and serve Onesimus as if he were Paul. The master now becomes the servant to the former slave. This is how Paul viewed the new relationship that has developed with Onesimus who is now a follower of Jesus and part of the family. The master-slave relationship seems to have come full circle because, in Christ, these differences cease to manifest themselves in the same way they do in society. Christians are bound by Christian love and by the example of Christ to serve rather than to be served.

The Christian faith may not have risen against the culture of slavery. The Apostles and the Church Fathers may not have preached against that culture or denounced it. Yet, they rose high above it by teaching masters how to treat slaves and slaves how to treat masters. Any possible reformation of that culture was only to come through the powerful transformative power of the Gospel and its live witness in that society.

Before we close this study, it is worth noting that a superb image can be drawn from this letter and the circumstances that triggered it. Philemon is said to resemble God the Father, and Onesimus the man who enslaved himself to sin. Enslaved humanity, in disobedience, robs God and becomes a fugitive. Paul is said to resemble Jesus, who reached down to humanity and, through the grace of adoption, turned the slave into a son. By virtue of his appeal and the offer to repay what the former slave owed, this adopted son may be accepted again in the house of God. In verse 18, Paul offered to pay Philemon for anything that Onesimus owed. Jesus did not only offer to pay. He paid indeed. The grace of Christ has turned us sinners and slaves to sin into sons and daughters of the Most High.

Philemon is the shortest book in the New Testament, but the practical lessons we can draw from its images are gigantic.

CHAPTER 28

Before the Cross of Jesus
Judas, Barabbas, and Simon

LUKE 14:27

Three men stand before the Cross of Jesus: Judas, Barabbas, and Simon. The name Judas has become associated with betrayal and shame. It is so abhorred and detested that rarely we hear of anyone giving their son this name. When we think of Judas, we immediately envision the Cross of Christ. It is as if Judas were the one behind it all. We may be tempted to think that were it not for him, Jesus would not have died, because Jesus would not have been betrayed.

Yet the fact is that Judas was the very reason for the cross and not the main character behind it. The sins of Judas were the reason why Jesus had to die, as foreordained by none other than God the Father.

Barabbas was a murderer, thrown in jail by the Roman authorities. The cross was meant for him. That was the way by which the Roman occupiers put murderers like Barabbas to death, except he was more than lucky on the day on which he would have been executed! The cross that was meant for him was the one that Jesus carried to Golgotha. Jesus carried it and was crucified on it on his behalf.

And then we have Simon the Cyrene who, according to the Gospel accounts of Mark, Matthew, and Luke, was forced to carry the cross behind Jesus. Luke says that the Roman soldiers "seized Simon from Cyrene" (Luke 23:26) and put the cross on him. Simon did not offer to help carry that cross. It was not a choice he made. Rather it was made for him. He could not possibly resist the Roman soldier who seized him and laid the cross on his shoulders.

Can we see ourselves reflected in any of these three characters? Or maybe in all of them?

Judas sold Jesus for thirty pieces of silver. He then betrayed him. Was that for political reasons? Was Judas, like many others, waiting for Jesus to launch an insurrection against the Romans? If so, Jesus failed to do that, and thus failed his expectations. Was that the reason why Judas sold Jesus out? We will never be able to answer that question. So how can we be like Judas? We neither sold Jesus nor betrayed him, at least not to that extent.

Nevertheless, there is one big reason for us to see ourselves in Judas. Inasmuch as the sins of Judas were the reason for the Cross, so are ours. It was not the Jews who put Jesus on the Cross, though some of them plotted to do that. It was not the Romans either, although they were the ones to put a crown of thorns on his head and drive nails in his hands and feet. It was our sins that put him there. Before the Cross, the first name for all of us becomes Judas.

Barabbas was a murderer. He was a Jewish zealot who had attempted to overthrow the Roman occupation. He was accused of treason and sentenced to death. So how can we be like Barabbas? We are not insurrectionists. We were never sentenced to death. But how about having someone crucified on the cross instead of us, in the same way that Jesus was nailed to the cross on which Barabbas was to be nailed?

According to the justice of God, we are all under the judgment, and all sentenced to die. We must pay for our sins and transgressions. By grace, and based solely on his love and mercy, God saw fit to have his only Son pay the penalty and offer the ultimate sacrifice so that whoever believes in him will escape eternal death. Barabbas escaped death. Jesus took his place, and by extension ours, when he bore his cross to Calvary and when the cross bore him.

As for Simon, it seems that this was his bad day, possibly his worst. He happened to be at the wrong place at the wrong time. All we know about him is that he was a native African born in Cyrene, which is in present-day Libya. How are we like him? We can be like Simon when we carry the cross as we follow the Master. Indeed, it is worth noting that Jesus called all his followers to "carry their cross"(Luke 14:27).

In the case of Simon, however, he was not carrying his own cross. He was carrying someone else's: the Cross of Jesus! Does that mean that at times we also will be called to carry not only our crosses but also those of others? Perhaps. In the cases of Judas and Barabbas, we do not have much choice since we are all sinners under divine judgment. But not so in the example of Simon! In this one case, we can choose to follow Jesus by carrying our own cross and other people's crosses, or we can decline. There are no Roman soldiers who will seize us and compel us to do that. The decision is completely ours.

Some crosses are heavier than others. Some crosses will cause us to stumble and fall. Others will cause us to doubt the love of God for us. And there will be situations in which we try to avoid having to carry any cross. Why allow ourselves to be in a situation in which we know full well that if we speak out for Christ, we will be shamed, insulted, and possibly persecuted? Better to avoid such situations and thus avoid having to carry the cross of our testimony for Christ!

In the end, though, a cross is a cross, be it heavy or light. It is not something we look forward to carrying. We convince ourselves that Jesus calls us to live for him and not die for him. He died for us, not vice versa. While that is perfectly true and correct, and while it is true that living for Jesus can be much harder than dying for him, true living for Jesus has a cost attached to it. Jesus put it this way: "A servant is not greater than his master. If they persecuted me, they will persecute you also" (John 15:20).

So, are we like Judas? We surely are, at least in one way. Are we like Barabbas? Here also, the answer is yes. How about Simon? It would be to our honor to resemble Simon in what he did on that fateful day. But that is a decision each one of us must make. No Roman soldier will force the cross on us. Rather, Jesus invites us to carry it and walk behind him. We walk behind him because he walked the road to Calvary ahead of us all! He set the example and asked us to do likewise.

CHAPTER 29

Ultimate Happiness
The Glory of God

EXODUS AND OTHER BOOKS

I imagine that if I were to ask a hundred churchgoers who know the Bible well what the secret is to humanity's ultimate happiness, I would get quite a collection of different answers. It is not that any would necessarily be wrong. And it is not that I claim to have the absolute, precise, and definitive answer to this question. However, in my estimation, after a rigorous and thoughtful study of the word of God, I believe that the secret to humanity's ultimate happiness is to glorify God. Not only do we exist to glorify God, but our true happiness is in the same. Allow me now to build my case for this claim.

There are very few themes that recur in the Bible as often as the glory of God. Here are just a few references from both the Old and the New Testaments.

Exodus 14:4, 17–19 talks about God's saying that he will gain glory for himself through Pharaoh and all his army. 1 Samuel 6:5 speaks of the priests and diviners of the Philistines saying, as they were returning the ark of the Lord, to give glory to the God of Israel. 1 Chronicles 16 says that the people are told to declare and ascribe glory to the Lord. Psalm 10:1 says even the heavens declare the glory of God. In Isaiah 43:7, God talks about his people being created for his glory. In Luke 2:14, when the angels appear to the shepherds at the birth of Jesus, the first part of their angelic song is "glory to God in the highest" (Luke 2:14). Human sin, as briefly defined by Paul in Romans 3:23, is to "fall short of the glory of God," meaning being unable to give glory to God. And in 1 Corinthians 10:31, Paul writes, "So whether you eat or drink or whatever you do, do it all for the glory of God."

The above are only a small sampling of the hundreds of times in Scripture in which the term "glory" is mentioned in reference to God. What does this say about God? Does this mean anything for us? And what does it really mean to glorify God?

Before we answer these questions, we must first unpack the term "glory" in a sincere attempt to understand it. To do that, we will go to a couple of words in Hebrew and to one word in Greek that were translated into the term "glory," and then seek to understand what they mean. But here again, it is not my intent to discuss every single meaning or shade of meaning that the words carry within them, because these are too many to count.

One prominent Hebrew term translated into glory is *khabod*. That word can also be translated as *honor, respect, and praise,* among other meanings. Another important Hebrew word is *hallel,* from which we get the word "hallelujah." *Yit-hallel*, a derivative of the verb *hallel,* was used in Jeremiah 9:23 and is rendered as "glory" in some English translations. In the NIV, it is rendered as "boast": "Let not the wise boast of their wisdom or the strong boast of their strength or the rich boast of their riches." Whether translated as "glory" or "boast," the general sense of this Hebrew verb in this verse is to delight in or to sing one's praises.

Then there is Exodus 14:4: "And I will harden Pharaoh's heart, and he will pursue them. But I will gain glory for myself through Pharaoh and all his army, and the Egyptians will know that I am the Lord." The latter part of this verse, namely that "the Egyptians will know that I am the Lord," adds a new dimension to our understanding of what God meant when he said that "He will gain glory through Pharaoh and all his army." That new dimension is the fact that God will reveal or declare something of himself that will cause the Egyptians to esteem, honor, and fear his majesty.

Paul writes that God revealed himself through the things that are made so that humanity knew God or knew of God, but even with that revelation, they did not glorify him. In other words, God's revelation in his creation was supposed to lead us to glorify God since we could see his attributes. Paul mentions God's eternal power and his divine nature as samples of these attributes. Yet humanity failed to give glory to God despite those self-revelations through his creative power. Revelation or declaration becomes the means by which the glory of God is exposed.

The Greek word translated as "glory" is *doxan*, from which we get the word doxology, meaning a formula of praise to God. Among the diverse meanings of this term are glory, opinion, and reputation.

If we now combine some of the meanings of the Hebrew terms and of the Greek term, we come up with this list of meanings of the term "glory:" honor, respect, praise, glory, opinion, and reputation.

So, when God is asking that he be glorified, what is he really asking us to do?

The short answer to this question would be to honor, respect, and praise him, to give a good opinion of him, and to speak well of his reputation. It also means to sing God's praises, to boast of him. We do that by revealing, declaring, uncovering, and testifying to one or more of his attributes. And since God is asking that he alone be glorified, by virtue of him being the creator and owner of all things, this means that nothing—whether in heaven, on earth, or beneath the earth—can receive any such praise, honor, or glory besides him.

This position explains why God went to great lengths in the Ten Commandments to say, "do not worship any other god, for the Lord … is a jealous God" (Exodus 34:14). In other words, worship is due to God alone. This explains the repeated warnings and the harsh judgment God would bring on Israel if they committed one very specific sin; namely, idolatry.

This now leads us to three important basic principles:

First, the most important requirement that God has of us is to glorify him: nothing and nobody else.

Secondly, since glorifying God is the most important requirement that God has of us, falling short of that is the most serious act of disobedience or mutiny that we can commit.

What does falling short of glorifying God mean? Historically, and especially since Paul defines sin as failing to glorify God or falling short of his glory, we have come to think of common acts such as lying, cheating, or lusting as sin. Yet, according to the verses above that discuss the glory of God, every time we keep quiet when people point to us and praise us, we are sinning against God because we allow ourselves, and not God, to be under the limelight. We allow ourselves to share in the limelight! Every time we succeed in doing something perceived by others to be good and revel in our success rather than give all the credit to God, we are sinning. Every time we pay our tithes or give money to the poor and pat ourselves on the shoulder, we are sinning. Obviously, these are but a small sample of situations in which we fall short. Sadly for us, it seems that we have been sinning much more often than we thought we were.

Lastly, since glorifying God is the most important requirement that God has of us, our ultimate happiness is to singularly glorify God.

I do not know if I have proven my claim or not. I may be wrong even calling it my claim, but I believe this is God's claim. Both his glory and our happiness are at stake. We do not serve a selfish or egoistic God. We serve a God who loves us and wants us happy. The only road to our ultimate happiness is by giving him all the glory—all the time, in all things, and under all circumstances. Therein lies our ultimate happiness!

Why Pray?
Becoming God's friend

I'd like to conclude this study by looking at prayer, specifically why we should pray. Even if there is nothing new or different I can add to the topic, I still hope my thoughts will be refreshing. For most of us, prayer is the means of beseeching or petitioning God for something. However, at times we pray without having an outspoken need in mind. Answers to the question "Why pray?" include:

1. We pray because God commands us to pray.
2. We pray because Jesus prayed.
3. We pray because prayer maintains our relationship with God.
4. We pray because prayer helps us to know the will of God and to submit to it.
5. We pray because through prayer we can be changed.
6. We pray because through prayer our circumstances can be changed.
7. We pray to offer thanks and resist temptation.
8. We pray because we have exhausted every other means available to us.
9. We pray because we need someone who can do something.
10. We pray because prayer is good for our troubled souls.

All of these answers, and many more, are biblically sound.

They are all based on the Word of God. They are also true and effective, both in the lives of men and women whose examples we have in Scripture and in the life of the church today.

The more I thought through the reasons for prayer, however, the more I felt that for the longest time, prayer has been seen as a means to an end. Eight out of the ten reasons above offer a specific end. Prayer in those eight situations is a means to one type of end or another. In the first answer offered, we pray as an act of obedience, and in the second, we pray following the example of Christ, but in the eight reasons that follow, there is an end to the means of prayer.

Here again, I want to make sure I am not being misunderstood. There is nothing wrong with prayer being a means to an end. The question is: What else could prayer be besides a means of having God hear us, answer us, and do something for us?

How about thinking of prayer as an end in itself? In other words, why not change our outlook and begin to consider the time we spend with the Lord in prayer simply as time spent with the Lord? This does not mean that such an outlook will do away with the more general outlook of prayer as a means. We will still pray to ask and to thank. We will still pray to change and have things change around us. We will still pray to intercede and to succeed. I am suggesting that we add a new element, a new outlook, and begin to think of prayer as an end in itself.

Let me explain. The four Gospels tell us that Jesus prayed quite often. However, we only rarely hear of Jesus using prayer as a means of supplication. His prayer in the Garden of Gethsemane was one such time. Most often, Jesus was seemingly only spending time with the Father.

In the field of evangelism, we hear talk of friendship evangelism. This methodology advances the idea of building relationships and developing friendships and then sharing the Gospel message. What I am suggesting might be called friendship prayer-ism! This outlook or notion is built around the basic premise that God is our friend, and, as friends we just spend time together.

To be friends with someone, one first has to have a relationship. Once a relationship is in place, a further investment of time is needed to turn that relationship into a friendship. Our relationship with God starts when we accept the sacrifice of his Son on our behalf on the Cross of Calvary. This is when we become reconciled to God through Christ and we become his children. But that doesn't mean we are friends with God. By the grace he bestowed on us we have become his adoptive children. He chose us to belong to him. But are we his friends? That choice is ours to make!

It is obvious that before we can begin to discover the depth and richness of communing with God as friends, we will need to work on our friendship with him. Friends meet over coffee, over lunch, over almost anything and nothing. Yes, nothing! They just enjoy being in each other's company. No one is asking favors or expecting anything. Friendship is not a means to an end. It is the end. The means is spending time together. Time with us is what God expects. Time with him is what we should plan on. Nothing more, and nothing less!

So why pray? The simple answer is to spend time with God. When we spend time in prayer with God, he may surprise us every now and then with marvels we did not expect. But that is not the point. The point is that when we spend time with God as his friend, our lives will be immeasurably enriched.

About the Author

Hanna Shahin was born in Palestine to Christian parents and was raised in the Old City of Jerusalem. He received Christ as his personal Savior in his late teens. He attended the American College in Jerusalem, before following God's calling that led him to the Baptist Seminary in Beirut, Lebanon. It was there that he met his future bride, Evelyn. Hanna began his full-time Christian ministry in July of 1971 and has since taught and ministered in the Middle East, Africa, Europe, Southeast Asia, and Australia. He co-translated and edited the first Greek Arabic Lexicon of the New Testament, and translated and produced the first Arabic version of *The Jesus Film*. Hanna pursued further education in Lebanon, Europe, and the United States, and holds undergraduate and graduate degrees in theology, philosophy, psychology, and biblical counseling, and a Ph.D. in missiology. Hanna spent more than twenty-six of his forty-eight years in ministry in international Christian broadcasting, during a large part of which he headed up the Arabic Ministry of Trans World Radio, while based in southern France. Hanna was ordained in 1988 as a minister within the Southern Baptist denomination. In January of 2005 he and his wife Evelyn founded Endure International, a disciple-making and church planting ministry, of which he serves as President. Hanna is the author of two books, *My Enemy … My Brother* and *The Master Disciple-Maker*. Hanna and his wife, Evelyn, have four sons, two grandsons, and two granddaughters.